Christianity
AND
ISLAM

GLOVER SHIPP

Christianity

AND

ISLAM

BRIDGING TWO WORLDS

COVENANT
PUBLISHING

www.covenantpublishing.com

P.O. Box 390 · Webb City, Missouri 64870
Call toll free at 877.673.1015
Library of Congress Cataloging-in-Publication Data

Shipp, Glover.
  Christianity and Islam: bridging two worlds / Glover Shipp.
    p. cm.
Includes bibliographical references.
  ISBN 1-892435-17-9 (pbk.)
  1. Missions to Muslims. 2. Islam—Essence, genius, nature. I. Title.

  BV2625 .S48 2002
  261.2'7—dc21
                                                        2002003362

DEDICATION

To the memory of
Ramón Lull, a Basque missionary
who in the 14th century attempted to convert
Muslims to Christianity.
In 1314, at more than 80 years of age
and while in another mission effort in
Muslim North Africa,
he was stoned to death.

ACKNOWLEDGMENTS

I am indebted to my professors at Fuller Theological Seminary; my colleagues in Brazil (and especially my publishing assistant, Helgir Girodo) . . .

To Dr. William Jones, retired professor of church history at Oklahoma Christian University; Dr. Robert Douglas, former missionary in Muslim countries and authority on the Muslim religion; Dr. Jack Evans, president of Southwestern Christian College, Terrell, Texas, and authority on the Black Muslim Movement; certain unnamed Muslim converts to Christianity . . .

To Felicia Moghbel, who has had extensive involvement for more than 20 years with Iranian Muslims in both the religious and political realms, and who read this manuscript for accuracy; and Steve Cable and John Hunter at Covenant Publishing for their encouragement and technical skills.

TABLE OF CONTENTS

Introduction

September 11, 2001, terror struck home against the World Trade Center, the Pentagon and Pennsylvania. Americans are asking *why* us? And *what* is Islam? Of special concern is the extremist level of Islam, often called Islamist Fundamentalism. We want to know more because we are woefully ignorant of Islam, in spite of the facts that Islam is the fastest-growing world religion and it purports a powerful presence throughout the United States and many other countries. James Beverley has written,

> Osama bin Laden, the world's most notorious terrorist, has handed Muslims everywhere their worst public-relations nightmare: September 11 as a picture, an embodiment, of Islam. Muslims now have to define themselves in relation to the day of infamy.

Later in the article: "Every judgment about Islam, all reaction to Muslim doctrine, and each Muslim-Christian encounter are now cast in light of the events of that dreadful day" (Beverley 2002:32).

Muslims are becoming our next-door neighbors at an ever-increasing rate. It is estimated that Islam now comprises at least 20% of the world's population. We need to know more about them and about their faith. Islam need not be considered a mysterious, impenetrable, or monolithic religion. On the contrary, it can be analyzed, understood, and answered. Strategies long overdue can be developed to successfully plant Christian beachheads on Islamic soil, some areas and sects of which are more receptive than others at this time in history.

Christianity and Islam answers the "why us" and "what is Islam" questions with an overview of this seemingly mysterious world religion. We will investigate Islam, its history, and its doctrine (Chapters 1, 4, 6, and 8). We will even explore the Qur'an (Koran) to some extent (Chapters 3 and 7). We will look briefly at Islamic terrorism and the mentality behind it (Chapter 9). And we will compare Islam with Christianity (Chapter 10). (You may wish to begin with Chapter 10, then go back to Chapter 1.) Finally, we will sound a call for courageous Christians to answer the increasingly great challenge that Islam represents in our nation and world. At the close of each chapter is a section entitled, "Bridging Two Worlds." The first part of this section is for reflecting on the Chapter. The second part contains suggested applications for bridge building. With God's help let us find ways to introduce Muslims to the ultimate Bridge between these two different worlds and between our world and heaven—Jesus Christ.

This book comes out of a history of research into world religions. Confronted with a confusing array of different religions while serving 18 years in Brazil and teaching visits to more than 40 other countries, I saw the need for exploring the major and minor religious movements around the globe. A first result was my intensive book in Portuguese, *Análise de Doutrinas* (Analysis of Doctrines), published in Brazil in 1985. I then taught courses on this subject and on world religions, both in Brazil and in universities and churches in the U.S., Nigeria, Kenya, India, Nepal, and elsewhere.

Then, in 1997, I presented a paper on Islam during the annual faculty colloquium at Oklahoma Christian University. To my surprise, it received the faculty research award for that year. I have continued to research world religions, including Islam. Currently I am completing a book on "Christ, the Church and Culture," which will include a section on Islam. Since the terrorist attacks of September 11, 2001 in New York City and Washington, D.C., I have been teaching courses specifically on Islam. In order to further my understanding of Islam, I am enrolled in a course by Professor Muhammad Wolfgang G.A. Schmidt, Berlin Free University.

Even with all of this background, I still understand only partially the Muslim mindset. However, perhaps the proverb, "In the country of the blind the one-eyed man is king," can apply here. If my partial knowledge helps the reader gain new insights into Islam, then this book will have been successful. Any progress will help, for we are way past due in coming to a better understanding of Islam. We not only need to know more about Islam, but also we need to build a bridge to share the gospel. Our attitude should be one of submission to God's will in sharing the good news to *everyone* outside of Christ.

Just a note about other matters in the book: References are cited parenthetically in the anthropological style, with the last name of the author, the date of the book, and the page number. The bibliography contains more complete information about these sources. For the reader's additional benefit, I have included a glossary of key words in Islamic studies and a list of Islamic countries, along with relevant maps. Also found there is an essay entitled, "Was Muhammad a Prophet or Founder of a Human Religion?" Spelling variations are due to translation difficulties out of the Arabic language and over 1,400 years of changing traditions or usage. Quotations from the Qur'an are from the English translation by Marmaduke Pickthall and approved by the Executive Council of His Highness Sultan-ul-Uloom Nawab Sir Mir Osman Ali Khan Bahadur, Nizam of Hyderabad and Berar.

Dr. Glover Shipp
Edmond, Oklahoma
May 2002

The Story of Two Worlds Begins

In the beginning God created the heavens and the earth. Now the earth was formless and empty, darkness was over the surface of the deep, and the Spirit of God was hovering over the waters (*Genesis 1:1-2*).

Then God said, "Let us make man in our image, in our likeness and let them rule over the fish of the sea and the birds of the air, over the livestock, over all the earth, and over all the creatures that move along the ground." So God created man in his own image, in the image of God he created him; male and female he created them (*Genesis 1:26-27*).

"And I will put enmity between you and the woman, and between your offspring and hers; hew will crush your head, and you will strike his heel" (*Genesis 3:15*).

The Lord had said to Abram, "Leave your country, your people and your father's household and go to the land I will show you. I will make you into a great nation and I will bless you; I will make your name great, and you will be a blessing. I will bless those who bless you, and whoever curses you I will curse; and all peoples on earth will be blessed through you" (*Genesis 12:1-3*).

1

Overview of Islam

The year is AD 622. Muhammad, an Arab camel-driver, trader, and manager of the estate of Khadija, a wealthy widow whom he had married, is fleeing for his life. With his wife; his kinsman, Abu Bakr, and his slave, Zaid, he is hurrying from Mecca to Medina, in the western Arabian Peninsula.

Through a series of revelations he reported to have received from the Angel Gabriel, he had announced to the people of his home city, Mecca, a new religion for the pagan Arabian tribes. With elements from Judaism and Christianity (in its developing form) he formulated a strictly monotheistic religion—"submission to Allah only." Al-ilah had been a principal god in the Arabian pantheon and the name is derived from the Canaanite word, El, and the Hebrew word, Elohim. He called his faith "Islam," which means *submission* or *surrender*.

When he presented his message in Mecca, he was at first ignored and then threatened with death. With his life at stake, he fled. In Medina, unlike Mecca, he and his new doctrine came to be accepted. From this tiny beginning Islam eventually spread from India to Spain, reaching temporarily into France and to the gates of Vienna, Austria, thus threatening the body of Europe itself. Following is a more detailed story of Arabia before Muhammad, his life, the development of Islam, and its history to the present time.

Arabia before Muhammad

A Mixed Racial Background

The Arabian Peninsula, located between the Red Sea and the Persian Gulf, has a long history. According to Noss and Noss, Sumerian, Babylonian, Persian, and Ethiopian peoples had entered Arabia (1994:580). They brought with them their polytheistic religions. Some of these, especially of Sumerian and Babylonian roots, elevated the moon god and the planet Venus.

The Ishmaelites

A major thread in the development of the Arabian peoples is found in the Book of Genesis. Ishmael, the oldest son of Abraham (by his wife's maid, Hagar), lived to the south of Canaan and is considered by Arabs to be their direct ancestor. Enmity began between Ishmael's line and that of Isaac's (the Israelites) in Abraham's tents and continues to the present time. Through Ishmael, the Arabian peoples not only believe Abraham to have been their major ancestor (Genesis 16 and 21), but also one of the great prophets of Islam.

Early Southern Arabia

We know relatively little of the subsequent history of the peninsula down to Roman times. Archaeology and other sources have confirmed that various kingdoms existed in the southern region in what are now Yemen and Oman. These developed along the trade routes from the east and were fueled financially by taxes imposed on caravans and by trading valuable spices grown in the region.

The first of these powers was the Minean, existing from about 1200 BC to 650 BC. The second was the Sabaean, founded in the 10th century BC and lasting until about 115 BC. It is thought that the queen of Sheba, who visited King Solomon, was in reality the ruler of Saba (1 Kings 10:1-13; see also Genesis 10:7). The third kingdom was the Himyarite, lasting from about 115 BC to about AD 525.

Early Northern Arabia

In Northern Arabia the earliest powerful kingdom was the Nabatean, which flourished from about 9 BC to AD 106 and extended all the way to Damascus on the north. Petra became its "mecca" of culture and education. The Nabatean script evolved into later Arabic, which was used in the Qur'an, the Muslim sacred book. Rome finally conquered the Nabateans in AD 106.

Overview of Islam

In the 4th century the Abyssinians spread into Arabia from northeastern Africa, bringing for awhile the Monophysite form of Christianity to an otherwise pagan tribal society. The Monophysites believed that Jesus' nature remained totally divine and not human even though He had taken on human form (although some have concluded that the controversial doctrine may have been more a misunderstanding of technical terms and not of theology). Judaism too came to Arabia at an early time, with Jewish merchants controlling much of the wealth of the peninsula.

Animism and Polytheism

Then in the 5th century the Persian Sassanid Empire gained control over southern Arabia. The remainder of the peninsula became fractured into warring nomadic tribes, all of which practiced forms of animism and polytheism. Each had its own tribal deity or deities, but believing that there was one supreme yet remote god ruling over all. As in classic animism in many other regions, animals and objects of nature were considered sacred. "There was a wide cult of sacred stones, supposed to contain divine power. Through rubbing, stroking, or kissing them one could, it was supposed, derive some of this power for oneself. Trees and springs . . . were also objects of veneration" (Smart 1996:288).

In addition to their animism, the Arabian tribes worshiped various celestial gods. One of these was *Allat*, the moon goddess, related to the mother goddesses of most of the ancient world. Then there were *al-Uzza*, the Planet Venus; and *Manat*, the goddess of fate, who controlled the life and destiny of people. "Al-Uzza in particular attracted an important sacrificial cult. Archaeologists have discovered traces of human sacrifice offered to her at an even earlier period. She was associated with the veneration of stone pillars . . . . " (Smart 1996:288).

The Ka'bah (or Ka'aba) Cube

The Quraysh (or Quraish) Tribe, into which Muhammad was born, lived in and around Mecca, and gave special reverence to al-Uzza. She became a prominent deity associated with the Ka'bah, a sacred structure that became a center for pilgrimage even in remote pagan times. The Ka'bah was a cubicle structure without decoration. It was built over a highly sacred black stone, still in place today and still reverenced by Muslims. Pilgrims kiss an exposed surface of it in their circumnavigation of the Ka'bah during their *hajj* (pilgrimage) to Mecca. Noss and Noss comment about this stone:

> Mecca offered the most conspicuous instance of veneration given to a stone—that given to the meteorite built into the corner of the holiest shrine in Arabia, the Ka'bah . . . . In some far past the people of that part of Arabia had been startled by the rush of a meteor . . . . Afterwards the awed inhabitants worshiped it, calling it "the black stone that fell from the heaven in the days of Adam."

> Bedouins came from far away, year after year, to sacrifice sheep and camels and to run the circuit of the stone seven times and kiss it, in the hope of heaven's blessing on them (Noss and Noss 1994: 583).

Within the Ka'bah were images of different deities. Meccans especially believed that the Ka'bah had been built by Abraham and his son Ishmael, their ancestral patriarch. His lineage is found in Genesis 25:12-18. According to Noss and Noss, one tradition related that the first Ka'bah was built by Adam from a celestial prototype (ibid.). *It is fascinating to note that Muhammad took over the Ka'bah and dedicated it exclusively to Allah, but that earlier pagan practices were retained.* Examples are circumnavigating the Ka'bah and kissing the sacred stone. For a monotheistic faith, this is a strange syncretism harking back to pagan times in Arabia. This is much like the church practice of renaming pagan holidays, giving them (at least on the surface) a Christian identity.

The Ka'bah is considered so sacred that only a Muslim can approach it. Even the air above it is sacred, so no aircraft is permitted to pass over it. All Muslim prayers worldwide are oriented toward it, as is the direction in which all mosques face.

Well of Zamzam

Near the Ka'bah was the holy well Zamzam, the waters of which were sacred to the pilgrims. It is still considered holy by Muslims, another example of utilizing prior pagan mentality. Tradition says that this is the same well that Hagar, Ishmael's mother, was led to and so Ishmael founded a community near it, the future Mecca. (See Genesis 21:9-21 for the story of Hagar's flight. However, the Genesis account says the well was located in the desert of *Beersheba*, in Canaan, *not* in the Arabian Peninsula.)

To this practice the Arabians added a tradition called the Lesser Pilgrimage, in imitation of Hagar's anguished search for water for her son. Later a Greater Pilgrimage was added. This required several days and included in its route various historical sites seen as significant by the tribes. Rituals included running back and forth between two sacred hills and other festivities to be discussed later. As in the above traditions, the idea of an annual pilgrimage also was taken over by Muhammad and given prominence in his religious calendar.

Mecca and the Quraysh (Quraish) and Khuza'a Tribes

Mecca was not only a religious shrine, tended by the Quraysh Tribe. It was also a thriving trade center over which two rival groups fought for control. These were the Quraysh and the Khuza'a. To complicate matters, the Quraysh was divided among twelve often-fighting clans, one of which was the Hashemite, Muhammad's clan. It was the most powerful and least inclined to civil strife.

Ludwig says that the people of Arabia were ignorant and in deep spiritual darkness, their minds filled with superstitions and barbarous thoughts. There was no central government. Each tribe was an independent entity and a law unto itself. Life was violent, with murder and robbery common, and the law of vendetta ruled. Ancient Arabs were immoral and drunken, to boot (Ludwig 1996:449, Esposito 1988:8).

This, then, was the condition of Arabia in AD 570, the year in which tradition claims Muhammad was born.

The Early Life of Muhammad

Muhammad's grandfather, 'Abd al-Muttalib, was the leader of the Hashemite(s) clan, which was prominent in Mecca. Soon, however, the Umayyad family dominated and the Hashemites lost their position of power (Ludwig 1996: 450).

Many Homes

One of his 10 sons, 'Abdallah, married and had only one child, Muhammad. 'Abdallah died soon thereafter. The infant was given to a Bedouin clan until he was five, so that he could learn the ways of the desert. Then he was restored to his mother, but she died shortly later. He lived with his grandfather for three years. When the grandfather also died, Muhammad's uncle, Abu Talib, the new head of the family, received him. Talib was a merchant who took his young charge with him on caravan trips.

The Widow, Khadija

As still a young man, Muhammad began to work for a wealthy widow, Khadija. She was so impressed with him that they soon married, even though he was 25 and she was 40. She gave him four daughters and three sons, the sons all dying in infancy (Esposito 1988:8).

Muhammad's Rise to Respect

Muhammad was now wealthy and held a high position among the people of Mecca. Muslim tradition states that miraculous signs surrounded his conception and birth. It claims that once two angels came and weighed his heart against those of his people, finding that his heart outweighed them all. Another tradition says that a Christian monk recognized Muhammad as God's messenger.

During the years following his marriage, Muhammad became an arbitrator and respected leader in Mecca. He became know as al-Ammin, the Trusted One (Esposito 1988:8). He was contemplative by nature and was deeply disturbed by the rivalry and bloodshed among the tribes. Once he was called upon to umpire an inter-tribal rebuilding of the Ka'bah and embedding of the sacred stone again in its place. Each tribe insisted that it be the one to place the stone. Muhammad solved the problem by placing the stone in a large sheet and instructing tribal leaders to lift the sheet by the corners, with Muhammad himself resetting it (Ishaq 1955. Translation by Guillaume 1988:84).

Muhammad's Encounters with Jews and Christians

During his earlier years Muhammad came into contact with both Jews and Christians. Arabia was a host for Catholics, Nestorians from Persia, and Monophysite Christians from Ethiopia. According to Noss and Noss, the most likely influences from these sources came to Muhammad through traders, along with merchants at the frequent commercial fairs in Mecca. Representatives of these faiths were in the habit of addressing those attending the fairs (Noss and Noss 1994:586).

The Qur'an indicates that these faiths aroused Muhammad's curiosity. Some of his acquaintances in Mecca were well read in both the Jewish and Christian traditions. Of major influence on his thinking were Waraqa, a cousin of Khadija, and the poet Umaiya. That Muhammad had prior knowledge, even though partial, of those religions is seen in his frequent references to and borrowing from their Scriptures in the Qur'an. As the Islamic writer Fazier Rahman puts it, "If Muhammad had not known 'historically' the materials of the Prophet's stories, he would have been at a complete loss to understand what the Revelation was saying to him" (1968:7). The Qur'an's dietary prohibitions read like the Law of Moses:

> Permitted to you is the beast of the flocks, except that which is now recited to you . . . . Forbidden to you are carrion, blood, the flesh of swine . . . the beast strangled, the beast beaten down, the beast

fallen to death, the beast gored and that devoured
by beasts of prey . . . . (Sûrah 5).

Messenger of God at Age Forty
As he grew older, Muhammad made regular visits to a
cave on Mount Hira, a few miles north of Mecca, to medi-
tate. He had lost his sons, a bitter blow to him. More and
more he retreated from the world to brood over his misfor-
tunes and the problems his fellow tribespeople faced. "Here,
in long periods of solitude, he contemplated his life and the
ills of his society, seeking greater meaning and insight. Here,
at the age of 40 during the month of Ramadan, Muhammad
the caravan leader became Muhammad the messenger of
God" (Esposito 1988:9).

Bridging Two Worlds

The Drawing Table

1. Where were you September 11, 2001? What was your first reaction to the terrorist attacks?
2. What did you think when the first news accounts named Muslim extremists as the perpetrators?
3. Share what is to you the most shocking aspect of the background/early history of Islam.
4. Compare and contrast Muhammad's hometown reception with that of Jesus. (Read Matthew 13:54-58; Mark 6:1-6.)
5. Discuss Muhammad's encounters with Christianity and Judaism. Did he have an adequate understanding of both? Why or why not?

Bridge-Building Tools

Begin your journal in a small, loose-leaf notebook for bridge building between Christianity and Islam. Divide it into at least five or six major sections corresponding to the "Pillars of Islam" (see Chapter 6, "Basic Muslim Beliefs").

Replace information you have compiled with new insights or strategies to answer each pillar. In the same notebook, begin to keep a prayer journal for your contacts with Muslims. The Voice of the Martyrs in Bartlesville, Oklahoma sends an annual prayer calendar with information about non-Christian countries. (You will find information on VOM in our Resource section.)

Two Sons of Promise?
Preempting God's Covenant

"Look up at the heavens and count the stars—if indeed you can count them." Then he said to him, "So shall your off-spring be." Abram believed the LORD, and he credited it to him as righteousness. He also said to him, "I am the LORD, who brought you out of Ur of the Chaldeans to give you this land to take possession of it" (*Genesis 15:5-7*).

Now Sarai, Abram's wife, had borne him no children. But she had an Egyptian maidservant named Hagar; so she said to Abram, "The LORD has kept me from having children. Go, sleep with my maidservant; perhaps I can build a fam-ily through her." Abram agreed to what Sarai said. So after Abram had been living in Canaan ten years, Sarai his wife took her Egyptian maidservant Hagar and gave her to her husband to be his wife (*Genesis 16:1-3*).

Then Sarai mistreated Hagar; so she fled from her. The angel of the LORD found Hagar near a spring in the desert; it was the spring that is beside the road to Shur . . . . Then the angel of the LORD told her, "Go back to your mistress and submit to her." The angel added, "I will so increase your descendants that they will be too numerous to count." The angel of the LORD also said to her: "You are now with child and you will have a son. You shall name him Ishmael, for the LORD has heard of your misery. He will be a wild donkey of a man; his hand will be against everyone and everyone's hand against him, and he will live in hostility toward all his brothers" (*Genesis 16:6b-12*).

"As for me, this is my covenant with you: You will be the father of many nations. No longer will you be called Abram; your name will be Abraham, for I have made you a father of many nations. I will make you very fruitful; I will make nations of you, and kings will come from you. I will establish my covenant as an everlasting covenant between me and you and your descendants after you for the genera-tions to come, to be your God and the God of your descen-dants after you" (*Genesis 17:4-7*).

2

Muhammad's Revelations — The Qur'an

During one of his periods of introspection Muhammad reported having received a visit from the Angel Gabriel, who told him, "Recite!"

Recite, in the name of thy Lord who created,
created man from a blood clot.
Recite: And thy Lord is the Most Generous,
who taught by the Pen,
taught Man that [which] he knew not . . . (Sûrah 96).

When the vision was ended, Muhammad was able to recite it perfectly. He was filled with fear and agitation. "He was both frightened and reluctant. Frightened by the unknown—for surely he did not expect such an experience. Reluctant, at first, because he feared he was possessed and that others would use such grounds and dismiss his claims as inspired by spirits, or *jinns*" (Esposito 1998:9). (Qur'an means "The Recital" or "Recitations.")

This reaction is recorded as part of Islamic tradition, as is Muhammad's despondent attempt to commit suicide. His message was reinforced, however, by his wife, who assured him that the message he had received was not from a demon, but from Allah. Tradition also records that Khadija's cousin, Waraqua ibn Qussay, played an important role in Muhammad's acceptance of his message and role:

Surely, by Him in whose hand is Waraqa's soul, thou art the prophet of this people. There hath come unto thee the greatest Namus (angel) who came unto Moses. Like the Hebrew prophets, Thou wilt be called a liar, and they will use thee despitefully and cast thee out and fight against thee (A. Guillerme, trans. 1955:107).

Continuing Revelations

Over the next 22 years (610-632) Muhammad continued to receive such revelations, which, it is claimed, he mem-
orized word for word. Noss and Noss note that "when it
began to appear that the strange experiences, in which rhap-
sodies in Arabic flowed across his lips, would continue to
occur spontaneously, without his willing them, he came to
believe that Allah was using him as a mouthpiece"
(1994:588). At last Arabia too had received a scripture "of
later date and greater authority than the scriptures of the
Jews and Christians" (ibid.).

Scribes later copied each revelation down. Muhammad
never arranged the revelations in any kind of order. In fact,
there is no evidence of a complete collection of the Qur'an
being made before Muhammad's death. Abu Bakr, the second caliph, commissioned Zaid ibn Thabit to collect the writings (al-Bukhari, Sahib n.d. Aukara, Turkey: Hilal Yarinlari, Vol.
6:476).

Uthman, the third caliph, obtained Zaid's copy and
ordered a further compilation. At that time there were at
least three variant editions of the Qur'an, each regarded by
some as authoritative. Uthman ordered all but his authorized
version destroyed (Ashurst and Masood 1998:criteria 2).

A final edition was developed with vowel markings and
published near the end of the ninth century. All copies since
have descended directly from that version (ibid.).

Structure of the Qur'an

The compilers' purpose in using uncommon vowel
markings was to remove all doubt as to meaning. Fry and
King say that no Muslim would ever think of tinkering with
the text, revising it, or speculating over it. For this reason it
has never been subjected to the higher criticism to which the
Bible has been subjected (1980:63).

The Qur'an is quite different from the Bible. It is not history, nor does it follow any chronology. It is not biographical or philosophical. Ellwood says that it is "a book or proclamation: proclamation of the oneness and sovereignty of God, of His coming judgment, of the need to submit to Him" (1996:338).

It is written in its entirety in poetic form, with the longest chapter, or *sûrah*, second, following a short introduction, and each of the following sûrahs, 144 in all, added according to the length of each. For this reason, some of the earliest revelations appear buried toward the end of the text. The sûrahs are named by their predominant themes and divided into verses (ayah or ayat, meaning "sign").

The Bible was recorded by more than forty authors over a thousand-year period, and the New Testament, recorded, as far as is known, by apostles or close associates of apostles during the first century. By contrast Muhammad recorded none of the Qur'an in writing, since he was reputedly unschooled, but it is attributed to him as having come directly to him from Allah through the Angel Gabriel.

Five Claims about the Qur'an

First, Muslims believe it to be in its entirety the infallible word of God—since the book is claimed to be the actual words of Allah, transmitted by Gabriel—a direct transcript of the original source that is preserved eternally in Heaven. As proof of this they use its nobility and the power of its poetry. "If we judge by the contents of the Qur'an, Muhammad certainly stands in the tradition of the great prophets, in the force and sincerity of his utterances and the experiences which backed them" (Smart 1996:290).

Second, it is claimed that the events of Muhammad's life and those of the Arabian peoples have not been mingled with the "Divine Verses" of the Qur'an, as in the case of the Bible. "The Qur'an is the pure word of God. Not one word therein is not divine. Not a single word has been deleted from its text. The Book has been handed down to our age in its complete and original form since the time of Prophet Muhammad" (Muhammad Mirza. E-mail message, mmirza@ee.eng.ohio-state.edu).

There is a serious problem with this affirmation, however. As we have pointed out, there were variant editions of the text in the early years following Muhammad, some of which are even accepted today by some Muslim groups. How can it be determined beyond question that the version normally accepted today is the true original? The third caliph, 'Uthman, rounded up most of the variant editions of the text and, after, it is thought, editing one version, declared it to be the pure text. Were he and his associates *infallible* in their determinations over the text?

Third, it is further claimed that the Arabic language is still in use after 1,400 years, thus preserving the original text of the Qur'an with its original meanings. So, it is concluded that the book that God revealed to Muhammad exists today without the *slightest* alteration in its vocabulary. A modern Arabic-speaking person "can comprehend the Holy Qur'an with as much proficiency as did the Arabs of 14 centuries ago" (Syed Abul 'Aala Muadoodi, from a speech recorded by Mirza).

Again, a question. Has not the Arabic language changed much in 1,400 years? The English of 500 years ago is difficult for the modern English speaker to follow. How much more the Celtic or Anglo-Saxon of 1,400 years ago? Without much help indeed it could not be understood. How, then, can it be affirmed so adamantly that the Arabic of 1,400 years ago can be perfectly understood today? "Living" languages change constantly. The Hebrew of the Old Testament and the koine Greek of the New Testament, "dead languages" for many centuries, tend to carry their original meanings much better than any living language would. Although we are not comparing similar languages, the question remains regarding the claim of an *unchanged* living language.

Fourth, Muslims claim that the Qur'an was eternally pre-existent. Almost from the beginning of Islam arguments have raged within the movement over whether or not the Qur'an was eternally pre-existent or was created by Allah when the need arose. The Mu'tazilites, an early sect of Islam, denied that the Qur'an was eternal and uncreated. "To suppose that it was uncreated and eternal [as many believed] would destroy the unity of God by setting up beside him something else co-eternal with him and this would be polytheism, which the Qur'an itself condemned" (Noss and Noss 1994: 610).

One serious paradox in all of this is that there were never any witnesses, apart from Muhammad, to the revelations that became the text of the Qur'an. The Bible states a principle about the need for a plurality of witnesses to establish any truth, foundational in law and society even today, even in Islamic countries: "A matter must be established by the testimony of two or three witnesses" (Deuteronomy 19:15b). " . . . take one or two others along, so that 'every matter may be established by the testimony of two or three witnesses'" (Matthew 18:16).

Despite this legal question, the Qur'an in its entirety hangs on the testimony of Muhammad only. Others copied and organized it, but no one else ever saw the angel or heard the recitations Muhammad affirmed to have heard.

The Qur'an is always read in Arabic during Muslim public worship and liturgical activities, because it is believed that translations cannot do justice to its poetry and truths. I can attest to the poetry part. Even a cursory reading of the text in English leaves much to be desired in poetic rhythm and style. No Muslim is permitted to do a paraphrase or private translation of the text. It must be read *exactly* as written in Arabic.

Fifth, Islamic scholars say that the Qur'an is the final revelation of God, superseding all previous revelations. This raises another question about the authenticity of the Qur'an—even if it contains serious discrepancies and historical fallacies, is it still divine revelation, never to be changed or tampered with in any way? (The Bible, even though it has come under the extreme scrutiny of Higher Criticism, has withstood any objections to its divine origin.) "The Holy Qur'an occupies a place of eminence in Arabic literature which has not fallen to the lot of any other book . . . . But we may say more and assert with confidence that the place so occupied has not been attained at any time by any book anywhere" (Mawlana Muhammad 'Ali 1950:50). Christians should be ready to give an answer when questioned about the Bible's authenticity, historicity, and genuineness, and from an Eastern mindset. Muslims may not listen to the typical Western "rational" apologetic. It will take concerted effort on our part to reason on their wavelength.

Muhammad explained his periodic changes in the text as "new revelations" that superseded older ones. One good example is the so-called Satanic Verses (Sûrah 53:21-23).

"Did you consider al-Lât and al-Uzzâ
And al-Manât, the third, the other?
Are yours the males and His the females?

That indeed were an unfair division!
They are but names which ye have named, ye and your fathers, for which Allah hath revealed no warrant . . . . "

As I understand it, the latter four lines were changed by Muhammad. Originally they read,

"Those were the swans exalted;
Their intercessions is expected;
Their likes are not neglected."

According to Watt, both versions are recited in public. Muhammad's explanation was that Satan had deceived him and had inserted the false verses without the Prophet's knowing it (Watt 1970:45).

Bridging Two Worlds

The Drawing Table

1.   Is there anything unusual about Muhammad's claim to have received revelations from an angel? (Read Colossians 1:16; compare with Acts 7:35, 38; Hebrews 1:4; 2:2; Revelation 1:1; 22:16.)
2.   What is one of the proofs Muslims offer to back the claim that the Qur'an came from God?
3.   How is the Qur'an different from the Bible?
4.   Discuss the problem of witnesses to the Qur'an.
5.   What are the "Satanic Verses"?

Bridge-Building Tools

Research the history of the English Bible. Gather key evidences for its authenticity and genuineness and add them to your notebook. (For example, consult the apologetic volumes by Josh McDowell starting with *Evidence that Demands a Verdict*.)

Find a way to contact Muslims in your community or Muslims as near to you as you can. Begin to pray for opportunities to meet and develop friendships with them.

Set up informal sharing times with your new friends and carefully examine the evidence for the Qur'an and for the Bible.

Two Lineages, One Lord
Ishmaelites, The Prophet, and Lordship

These are the names of the sons of Ishmael, listed in the order of their birth: Nebaioth the firstborn of Ishmael, Kedar, Adbeel, Mibsam, Mishma, Dumah, Massa, Hadad, Tema, Jetur, Naphish and Kedemah. These were the sons of Ishmael, and these are the names of the twelve tribal rulers according to their settlements and camps. Altogether, Ishmael lived a hundred and thirty-seven years. He breathed his last and died, and he was gathered to his people (*Genesis 25:13-17*).

"I will raise up for them a prophet like you from among their brothers; I will put my words in his mouth, and he will tell them everything I command him. If anyone does not listen to my words that the prophet speaks in my name, I myself will call him to account. But a prophet who presumes to speak in my name anything I have not commanded him to say, or a prophet who speaks in the name of other gods, must be put to death." You may say to yourselves, "How can we know when a message has not been spoken by the LORD?" If what a prophet proclaims in the name of the LORD does not take place or come true, that is a message the LORD has not spoken. That prophet has spoken presumptuously. Do not be afraid of him (*Deuteronomy 18:18-22*).

The earth is the Lord's, and everything in it, the world, and all who live in it; for he founded it upon the seas and established it upon the waters. Who may ascend the hill of the LORD? Who may stand in his holy place? He who has clean hands and a pure heart, who does not lift up his soul to an idol or swear by what is false. He will receive blessing from the LORD and vindication from God his Savior. Such is the generation of those who seek him, who seek your face, O God of Jacob (*Psalm 24:1-5*).

The LORD says to my Lord: "Sit at my right hand until I make your enemies a footstool for your feet" (*Psalm 110:1*).

3

Evolution of the Qur'an and the Ahadith

Surâh 1 opens the text with these words:

1. In the name of Allah, the Beneficent, the Merciful. 2. Praise be to Allah, Lord of the Worlds, 3. The Beneficent, the Merciful. 4. Owner of the Day of Judgment. 5. Thee (alone) do we worship; Thee (alone) we ask for help. 6. Show us the straight path, 7. The path of those whom Thou hast favored; Not the (path) of those who earn Thine anger Nor of those who go astray (from English translation by Marmaduke Pickthall).

Smart notes that it is possible to discern phases in the composition of the text:

Modern critical scholars are inclined to the view that there were three phases. In the first phase Muhammad was at Mecca, trying to summon men to a recognition of the worship of Allah. In the second phase, covering the last years at Mecca and the first years of his residence in Medina, Muhammad incorporated into his revelations elements drawn from Judaism and Christianity.

In the third phase the revelations indicated a hardening of attitude toward these latter faiths and the final triumph of a distinct teaching (Smart 1996:290).

The Qur'an and the Old Testament

Many sections of the Qur'an utilize extensive historical passages from the Bible, but with notable changes. For instance in Sûrah 7:13-19, the story of Moses' leadership of the Israelites out of Egypt and toward the promised land is found, but with few of the laws given by God. Emphasis is placed on proving the oneness of God to Pharaoh and punishing Israel for substituting a golden calf for true worship to God. (See Ali 1992:373-390 for the entire sequence and the emphases given to it in the Qur'an.) It therefore appears that selective use was made of the Old Testament to prove a specific point, with little attention given to the precise facts of the source material. However, since Muhammad's only exposure to Biblical accounts were oral traditions, and the Bible was not translated into Arabic until after his death, *some* of the differences are understandable.

The Qur'an and the New Testament

The New Testament also enters into the Qur'an, but with considerable modification. For instance, Jesus' statement to the apostles, "No one knows about that day or hour, not even the angels in heaven nor the Son, but only the Father" (Matthew 25:36), or "It is not for you to know the times or dates the Father has set by his own authority" (Acts 1:7), is presented in the Qur'an in this way, with no reference to Christ:

> They ask thee about/ The (final) hour—when/ Will be its appointed time?/ Say: "The knowledge thereof/ Is with my Lord None but He can reveal/ As to when it will occur" (Ali 1992:398).

The Muslim version of the birth of John the Baptist and the virgin birth of Jesus are found in Sûrah 19. The story of Mary and Jesus reads as follows:

> 16. And make mention of Mary in the Scripture, when she had withdrawn from her people to a chamber looking East. 17. And had chosen seclusion from them. Then We sent unto her Our Spirit and it assumed for her the likeness of a perfect man. 18. She said: "Lo! I seek refuge in the Beneficent

One from thee, if thou are God-fearing." 19. He said: "I am only a messenger of thy Lord, that I may bestow on thee a faultless son." 20. She said: "How can I have a son when no mortal hath touched me, neither have I been unchaste?" 21. He said: "So (it will be)." The Lord saith: "It is easy for Me. And (it will be) that We may make of him a revelation for mankind and a mercy from Us, and it is a thing ordained." 22. And she conceived him, and she withdrew with him to a far place. 23. And the pangs of childbirth drove her unto the trunk of the palm-tree. She said: "Oh, would that I had died ere this and had become a thing of naught, forgotten!" 24. Then (one) cried unto her from below her, saying: "Grieve not! Thy Lord hath placed a rivulet beneath thee, 25. And shake the trunk of the palm-tree toward thee, thou will cause ripe dates to fall upon thee. 26. So eat and drink and be consoled. And if thou meetest any mortal, say: 'Lo! I have vowed a fast unto the Beneficent, And may not speak this day to any mortal.'" 27. Then she brought him to her own folk, carrying him. They said: "O Mary! Thou hast come with an amazing thing. 28. O sister of Aaron! Thy father was not a wicked man nor was thy mother a harlot" 29. Then she pointed to him. They said: "How can we talk to one who is in the cradle, a young boy?" 30. He spake: "Lo! I am the slave of Allah. He hath given me the Scripture, and hath appointed me a Prophet, 31. And hath made me blessed wheresover I may be, and hath enjoined upon me prayer and almsgiving so long as I remain alive. 32. And (hath made me) dutiful toward her who bore me, and hath not made me arrogant, unblest. 33. Peace on me the day I was born, and the day I die, and the day I shall be raised alive!" 34. Such was Jesus, son of Mary: (this is) a statement of the truth concerning which they doubt. 35. It befitteth not (the Majesty of) Allah that He should take unto Himself a son. Glory be to Him! When he decreeth a thing, He saith unto it only: "Be! and it is."

We see from this passage that the text confuses Mary with Miriam, the sister of Moses and Aaron, since their names were the same in Hebrew. Also, some of the facts of the New Testament narration were changed and Jesus' being the Son of God was totally negated.

However, Muslims hold Jesus in the highest regard, the greatest of the Great Prophets, next to Muhhamad, who they say took His place as the highest of the prophets. Miller comments on the Qur'an's teaching about Jesus:

> It states that he healed the sick cleansed lepers, gave sight to the blind, raised the dead to life, and brought down from heaven a table furnished with food (Sûrah 5:110,116). Jesus in the Qur'an is called the "Messiah," the "Word of God" and a "Spirit from God," . . . . But he must not be called "son of God," generally understood in a physical sense, and he must not be worshiped as a god (Sûrah 4:169) . . . . The Qur'an says that Jesus "will be illustrious in this world and in the next . . . ." (Sûrah 3:40). No other prophet, not even Muhammad, is praised as highly in the Qur'an as is Jesus Christ (Miller n.d.:48-49).

Yes, the Qur'an *honors* Jesus highly, but from my research, I find that Jesus is not highly elevated today in the Islamic world. In fact, He appears to be largely ignored.

In a misdirected effort to honor Jesus, the Qur'an insists that the Jews did not crucify Him. "They slew him not nor crucified him, but it appeared so to them" (Sûrah 4:157). Muslim scholars explain that God performed a miracle and spared Him, causing someone else, possibly Judas or one of the other disciples, to be placed on the cross in His stead (Miller n.d.:49). One names Simon of Cyrene as the one crucified.

Islam is built on a premise of revelation. God has spoken to His prophets. To some of these He also gave books.

According to Muslim tradition, these books are 104 in number. In the Qur'an there is reference to the *Torat* or *Taurah* (Books of Moses), the *Suhuf* (Books of the Prophets), the *Zabur* (Psalms of David), the *Injil* or *Injeel* (Gospel of Jesus), and the Qur'an itself. They believe that Adam, Noah, Abraham, and other prophets also gave us books, but these have been lost. Miller comments, "All of these are the Word of God . . . . However, when God gives a new book to one of the Great Prophets, He thereby abrogates the previous books" (Miller n.d.:52).

Therefore, since the Qur'an is the final Book, all before it are no longer valid. The Qur'an alone is sufficient and only its commands are binding. This ignores the clear Bible statement that Christ's Word would never pass away (Matthew 24:25).

Regarding its affirmations as to the absolute accuracy of its prophecies, Sûrah 30:3-4 says that the Romans would defeat the Persians. Rome had earlier defeated the Persians, but this was some time before the lifetime of Muhammad. Centuries later the Seljuk Turks, who conquered and devastated Jerusalem, defeated the Byzantine Empire, successor of the Roman Empire. So we see that this prophecy was certainly wrong.

Muhammad, God's Greatest and Final Prophet

To all Muslims Muhammad is the Prophet and Messenger above all others, including Jesus. It might be accurately said that he is **The Prophet**. In the Qur'an it is stated that Jesus announced the coming of an apostle whose name would be Ahmad (Sûrah 61:6). This they affirm to be Muhammad, since the two words come from the same Arabic root. Thus they assert that to believe in Muhammad is to be obedient to the command of Jesus to accept Muhammad, which Christians refuse to do.

Through the entire text of the Qur'an, the Messenger, Muhammad, is constantly mentioned. He is given all authority and those who do not listen to him will be cursed forever. One of many examples will serve: "And of them are those who vex the Prophet and say:/ He is only a hearer. Say: a hearer of good for you,/ who believeth in Allah and is true to the believers,/ and a mercy for such of you as believe./ Those who vex the messenger of Allah,/ for them there is a painful doom" (Sûrah 9:61). The Muslim mystic Hallaj wrote, referring to Muhammad: "All the Lights of the Prophets proceeded from his Light; he was before all, his name the first in the Book of Fate; he was known before all things and all being, and will endure after the end of all" (cited in Miller n.d.:50).

Not only is he considered the first of all, but also the Perfect Man, a sinless being. His example should be followed, according to Muslim tradition, in all things—eating, personal care, marriage, relationship to friends and enemies, worship, government, and war. The name of "the Apostle" is constantly on the lips of the devout.

For a religion that is strictly monotheistic, the elevation of Muhammad to a nearly godlike level strikes me as at least bordering on idolatry. And another problem: It was reported that Muhammad had a foreign lover of whom his wives disapproved, so he divorced them and continued to live with her. Do Muslim leaders really want the devout to follow that kind of example? It is historically recorded that he had at least 11 wives. Was he a man? If so, he was a sinner, for God's Word says that there is no righteous person, but that all have sinned (Psalm 14:1-3).

Moral and Social Teaching in the Qur'an

The Qur'an deals in great part with faith in the one God, Allah, but also considers many topics of a moral and social nature. For instance, a man who divorces his wife is to either take her back on equitable terms or free her on equitable terms. He is not to take a wife back to injure her or take undue advantage of her (Sûrah 2:231). Men are permitted a plurality of wives. They are never to shed the blood of their Muslim brothers, yet they do in such sectarian wars as that between Iraq and Iran. They are not to turn their own people from their homes (Sûrah 2:84). Yet they do.

Relationship to Christians and Jews

At first Christians and Jews were respected as "People of the Book." Later on, however, the text condemns them, and especially Christians, for having called anyone a son of God, thus impinging on the absolute oneness of Allah himself.

The Jews call "Uzayr" a son of God,/ and the Christians call Christ the Son of God./ That is a saying from their mouth:/ (In this) they but imitate/ What the unbelievers of old used to say./ Allah's curse be on them: how they are deluded/ Away from the Truth! . . . . / And (they take as their Lord)/ Christ the son of Mary;/ Yet they were commanded/ To worship but one God:/ There is no god but He (Ali 1992:446).

Jesus is the greatest of all stumbling blocks to the Muslims. This is due in part to the emphasis in the Qur'an on strict monotheism. It is due in part to Muhammad's misunderstanding of the nature and place of Christ as he saw the Savior in the light of what was mostly oral Christian doctrine of his day. It is due in part to the mistaken idea that there are three gods in Christianity. No, there is but one. He is manifested in the Bible in three persons—the Father, the Son, and the Holy Spirit. This should not be so difficult to understand. The analogy of water makes it clear. Water comes in three forms—liquid, solid, and vapor—yet it is still water. God is in three natures, yet is one. Jesus declared, "I and my Father are one" (John 10:30). So they are one, not separate gods, as Muslims mistakenly understand us to teach.

In downgrading Christ to the level of *a* prophet, they strip their religion of any Savior and Mediator. Apart from Christ there is no salvation, for anyone (Acts 4:12). All of their good works notwithstanding, Muslims are not saved. Moreover, the Bible says they are cursed of God and have no eternal life (1 John 5:1-12). In fact, John says they make Christ a liar. Since they believe Him to be second only to Muhammad as a prophet and declare that no prophet can lie, they are on the horns of a dilemma on this point. If Jesus says that He is the Son of God, is He lying or telling the truth? None of us is saved by works but by the grace of God through the One Mediator appointed by God, Jesus Christ.

The Ahadith and Other Supplements to the Qur'an

After the Qur'an had been finally determined in the form it has today, another important body of religious literature was added to it as a supplement. This is the *Ahadith* (from the Arabic, meaning "stories" or "narratives"). As time passed other supplements were created, many of them listings of judicial decisions over the centuries, much as the Babylonian Mishna, of Jewish tradition. There were also four different schools of Islamic thought, all contributing to the literature of the movement.

The Nature and Purpose of the Ahadith

Fry and King describe the Ahadith as "stories about the Prophet's works and deeds, and many of them, recounted by people who actually knew Muhammad, are regarded as authentic" (Fry and King 1980:65). The Ahadith also contained information about the life, habits, and daily comments of Muhammad.

Much more than the Qur'an, the Ahadith has been subjected to many additions and deletions over the centuries. The task of separating genuine from spurious Ahadith has always been a major task of Muslim scholarship, according to Fry and King (ibid.). Noss and Noss note, "As traditional Islamic scholarship itself points out, there was some invention or fabrication" (Noss and Noss 1994:605). It was two centuries later that any effort was made to filter the thousands of traditions that had arisen. Abu Huraira, one of Muhammad's companions, alone recorded 5,300 traditions. A woman historian, A'isha, wrote down 2,210 traditional stories. Some of these historians appear to have been too voluble and too precise in their long-term memory to have much credibility.

The most highly regarded Ahadith is that of al-Bukhari, a Persian who collected 100,000 stories attributed to Muhammad, sifting them down to 7,275. This collection ranks next to the Qur'an in importance. Five other collections are also treasured as canonical books.

Books of Islamic law

The Ahadith are not the only collections extant. Four schools of Islamic law came into being. These will be discussed later, but suffice it here to say that collections by the founders of two of these schools, Malik ibn Anas and Ahmad ibn Hanbala, have been given special regard in Muslim doctrine and law.

In addition, we will find later that decisions made by groups of Muslim leaders, by consensus, have the weight of law and are recorded in legal works. There are also commentaries on the Ahadith and other collections. Out of these have come the "genuine" traditions that are the basis of Sunnah, or Custom, of traditional Islam.

In more recent times have come doctrinal works, tracts, movies, films, and popular books on Islam, as the movement has become more evangelistic.

Bridging Two Worlds

The Drawing Table
1. How did Muhammad use the Old Testament in the Qur'an?
2. What are some discrepancies in the account of Mary and Jesus?
3. How do Muslims view Jesus today?
4. Discuss the claim that Jesus foretold Muhammad.
5. Explain the misunderstanding that Christianity has three Gods.

Bridge-Building Tools
Compile information from the early history of Islam regarding Muhammad's contact with Jews and Christians. Write down key points that you can share with other Christians in a small group or Bible class. Pray for ways in which you can work these concepts into conversations with Muslim friends that will help in understanding each other's faith.

One Messiah for Two Worlds
The Messiah Foretold and the Coming of Jesus

We all, like sheep, have gone astray, each of us has turned to his own way; and the LORD has laid on him the iniquity of us all. He was oppressed and afflicted, yet he did not open his mouth; he was led like a lamb to the slaughter, and as a sheep before her shearers is silent, so he did not open his mouth. By oppression and judgment he was taken away. And who can speak of his descendants? For he was cut off from the land of the living; for the transgression of my people he was stricken. He was assigned a grave with the wicked, and with the rich in his death, though he had done no violence, nor was any deceit in his mouth. Yet it was the Lord's will to crush him and cause him to suffer, and though the LORD makes his life a guilt offering, he will see his offspring and prolong his days, and the will of the LORD will prosper in his hand (*Isaiah 53:6-10*).

A record of the genealogy of Jesus Christ the son of David, the son of Abraham: Abraham was the father of Isaac, Isaac the father of Jacob, Jacob the father of Judah and his brothers, ... and Jacob the father of Joseph, the husband of Mary, of whom was born Jesus, who is called Christ (*Matthew 1:1, 2, 16*).

Now Jesus himself was about thirty years old when he began his ministry. He was the son, so it was thought, of Joseph, the son of Heli, ... the son of Jacob, the son of Isaac, the son of Abraham, the son of Terah, the son of Nahor, ... the son of Enosh, the son of Seth, the son of Adam, the son of God (*Luke 3:23, 34, 38*).

In the beginning was the Word, and the Word was with God, and the Word was God. He was with God in the beginning. Through him all things were made; without him nothing was made that has been made . . . . He came to that which was his own, but his own did not receive him. Yet to all who received him, to those who believed in his name, he gave the right to become children of God—. . . . The Word became flesh and made his dwelling among us. We have seen his glory, the glory of the One and Only, who came from the Father, full of grace and truth (*John 1:1-5, 11-14*).

4

Division in the Ranks of Islam

Islam began as an insular movement. That is, it was limited to the Arabian culture, language, and tribes. However, it expanded rapidly to incorporate many other peoples of differing cultures, worldviews, and languages. This created a challenge to the early leaders of the movement. New situations arose. New leaders arose. New ideas were presented. As with all religious movements, over a period of time differences of opinion, philosophy, culture, and even politics created division in Islam.

Separation into Sects

Early in its history Islam separated into sects. The first controversies arose over *succession* because Muhammad named no successor! Some argued that only his family or his clan should furnish the next head of the movement. Others argued that anyone from among his closest associates could become the leader. An impasse developed.

To solve the issue, his kinsman 'Ali was named *caliph*, or successor. Others in the movement watched him closely, to see if he would be as decisive as Muhammad. When he used arbitration, rather than authority, 12,000 warriors left him. These became know as *Kharijites* (secessionists or seceders). Noss and Noss say:

> Viewing with hostile eyes the political developments occurring behind the scenes among the Muslim leaders, this group concluded bitterly that the only sure way of getting the right caliph was to select the best qualified person, not necessarily someone from the Prophet's family or just his tribe (Noss and Noss 1994:606).

Before long the ill will produced by this schism resulted in a mini-war, with many of the more radical Kharijites killed. Their chief opponents were the Murjites, who believed that only Allah can judge who is a true Muslim (and a true leader of the faith).

With the rapid expansion of Islam from Arabia to North Africa and the Near and Middle East, Muslims suddenly faced new situations and cultures. In these the Qur'an proved to be less applicable than it had been in Arabia. So appeals were made to the *sunnah* (behavior or practice) of Muhammad. If that procedure proved inconclusive, leaders looked to the practice of the Medina community after Muhammad's death. If that step didn't resolve the question, then they resorted to a process called *quyas*. This was a decision made by drawing an analogy based on Qur'anic principles and on any pertinent Medina precedents. Such a process might involve *ijtihad*, which is the exercise of reason (Noss and Noss 1994:606-607).

However, it must be noted here that reason or logic has its limitations. Much depends on the thought processes and the prior points of view of those arriving at a decision. No logic is perfect in the hands of fallible humans.

Those following the quyas procedure for their doctrinal and practical position are called *Sunnis*. They represent the majority of Muslims today and tend to be less dogmatic, fundamentalist, and militant than other branches of Islam. In approaching Muslims, it would appear wise to contact Sunnis first and use reason, analogies, and other methodology from their own experience to discuss Christianity with them.

Much attention was given in the centuries following Muhammad's era to Islamic law and its interpretation. Since there was little distinction between law and religion, the courts tended for centuries (and in some countries still do) to be religion-based rather than civil-based.

Out of Islamic theological and civil law came the *shar-i'ah*, a system calling for a theocratic government over Islamic nations. Fundamentalists still call for shari'ah-based legal systems—a return to the structure by which early Islam was ruled. Saudi Arabia, Iran, Iraq, Sudan, and other nations have announced their intention to be purely Islamic in all details of government and society. This can be seen in the positions of the Taliban Party in Afghanistan. It was radically fundamentalist, denying women education and other rights, forcing them to be totally covered in public, and wishing to rule the country with an iron hand.

However, in more open Islamic societies, women are much better educated and are no longer satisfied with meekly submitting to male domination in every realm. Nor do they gracefully submit to using a shapeless gown and veil in public.

The Four Schools of Islamic Law

Out of the religion-law partnership (and at times controversy) came four schools of law. These were the *Hanifite, Malikite, Shaf'ite* and *Hanbalite*.

The first chronologically was the *Hanifite*, founded in the latter part of the eighth century by Abu Hanifa, a Persian scholar. His general practice, say Noss and Noss (1994:608), was to largely ignore the Ahadith, taking principles from the Qur'an and applying them by analogy or reason to the different setting that he found in his homeland, Iraq. Hanifite principles of law and logic have been followed by Muslims in Iraq, Iran, Pakistan, India, and Central Asia.

The second, the *Malikite*, was founded in Medina by Malik ibn Anas at some time near the end of the same century. He interpreted laws and rites through careful analysis of both the Qur'an and the Ahadith. He relied heavily on *ulama* (consensus of opinion). The public good was considered in difficult decisions. The Malikite School is followed in North Africa, upper Egypt, and eastern Arabia.

The third school in time was the *Shafi'ite*, founded by al-Shafi'i, an Arab of the Quraysh Tribe who had been born in Persia. He arrived at a blending of the earlier schools by citing four sources of Islamic law—the Qur'an, the Ahadith, consensus of the Muslim community (especially the jurists), and reasoned analogy.

The fourth school is the *Hanbalite*, founded in Baghdad by Ibi-Hanbal. He placed strict conservative emphasis on the Qur'an only. For this he was imprisoned and persecuted by the more liberal Islamic court at Baghdad. His school is followed throughout Saudi Arabia.

Divisions Resulting from Succession

We have mentioned that Muhammad named no successor. This lapse created controversy over who should follow him as *caliph* (leader of the movement), whether a member of Muhammad's family or a close associate of the Prophet. The leadership finally decided that Abu Bakr, a close friend and father-in-law of the Prophet, and one of the first converts, should succeed him as caliph. This position, notes Ludwig, was a combination of chief executive, military commander-in-chief, judicial leader and director of worship, called *imam* (1989:456). The only honor denied him was being named prophet, since it was believed that Muhammad was Allah's final prophet.

Abu Bakr led Islam for only two years, but showed much skill in consolidating the Arabian tribes in the faith, collecting scattered sûrahs of the Qur'an and punishing apostasy. He was followed by 'Umar and 'Uthman, also early converts who, in 20 years, turned Islam into a world religion. During their leadership Islamic military forces subdued Jerusalem, Syria, Persia, Asia Minor, Egypt, and North Africa. Dedicated and disciplined Arabian horsemen had little difficulty in carrying out their jihad against the "infidels."

Because these two caliphs considered Jews and Christians as "People of the Book," the two groups were treated with a fair degree of toleration. However, the caliphs did impose Islamic law and required a head tax from both Jews and Christians. Their mentality was to establish theocratic rule in which all aspects of life were to be governed by the code of Islam.

The story culminates, then, in the rule of Islam as a unified worldwide *ummah* (brotherhood), whether that is called the caliphate or the imamate. This is, of course, an ideal that has never been completely achieved. But it is the goal set forth in the Muslim story that the ummah become the ideal human society, in which Muslims as representatives of true humanity submit their lives totally in accordance with God's will as revealed through the Prophet Muhammad (Ludwig 1989:457).

This ideal condition, to the thinking of the leadership, could only be reached through the establishment of an Islamic state. All laws of this state, whether civil, social, or religious, and in both the public and private sectors, would be based solely on the Qur'an (ibid.).

Expansion of the Islamic Empire

In order to realize this ideal state on a grand scale, it was necessary to bring other nations and peoples into the Islamic family. So military conquest and other means attained the goal of world domination in an amazingly short period of time.

By the year AD 750 Islam had spread as far west as Spain, remaining in power in much of that country until 1492, when it was expelled by Ferdinand and Isabella. To the northwest expansion had been stopped by the Frankish ruler Charles Martel at the Battle of Tours in southern France in 732, thus preventing the forced conversion of Europe to Islam. To the east Islam had surrounded the Caspian Sea and had gone as far as present Pakistan.

Armed conquests continued at a rapid pace until about 1500, when Islam controlled North Africa southward to the Sahel and along the east coast of Africa as far south as Mozambique and Madagascar. To the northeast it had taken Greece, Albania, the southern Slavic states, Turkey, much of what is now western and central Russia, and the Ukraine. To the east it had spread throughout much of India and down into Malaysia and Indonesia. (For additional information on this remarkable expansion in a 750-year period, see Ludwig 1996:456.)

The Origin of the Shiites

'Ali, Muhammad's cousin and husband of his daughter, Fatima, was thought by many Muslim leaders to be the rightful heir to the vacancy left by the Prophet's death. However, he and his son Huseyn were assassinated. This only intensified the outcry of the Shiites (from shi'a, or faction). The leaders they advocated, called *imams* rather than *caliphs*, were direct descendants of Muhammad's family.

> Most Shi'ites hold that there were twelve imams before the final one and he disappeared, to return sometime in the future. Shi'ites look to these imams for special guidance, since the light of Muhammad was passed on to the Imam 'Ali and from him to the rest of the imams (Ludwig 1996:457).

The Shiite sect has continued to the present time, concentrated primarily in Iran and numbering about 15 percent of all Muslims. It is militant in attitude and holds that all other branches of Islam are in error, following after false caliphs. One of the reasons for the continual enmity between Iran and Iraq is over this very question, Iran being Shiite and Iraq Sunni.

Further Divisions among the Shiites

The Shiites themselves divided into sects, the more important of these being the *Zaidites*, the *Twelvers*, and the *Ismailites*.

First, the Zaidites approximate most closely the Orthodox Muslim faith. They claim that 'Ali freely gave his allegiance to the first two caliphs, Abu Bakr and 'Umar.

Therefore they, with him, should be recognized as legitimate. They "all agree that the Ummayyads who succeeded 'Ali were usurpers of the lowest kind: they were and are accursed" (Noss and Noss 1994:622). The Zaidites have maintained a succession in Yemen, Morocco and other locations.

Second, the Twelvers constitute the majority of the Shiites. They believe that the 11th imam, Muhammad al-Muntazar, disappeared as a child, leaving no son. However, Allah would not allow the divine line of imams to disappear, so the 11th imam will reappear in the fullness of time to bring in a glorious new era of righteousness and peace. Almost all of the Iranians are Twelvers and Iran, not coincidentally, is Islamic by government decree.

Third, the Ismailites are a large body of Shiites found in India, Pakistan, East Africa, Syria, Lebanon, and Yemen. Their loyalty is to Ismail, the first son of the sixth imam. This son was set aside, to them unjustly, as the seventh imam. They believe that he will return as the longed-for *Mahdi*, or restorer of peace and righteousness. Their interpretation of the Qur'an is allegorical, with great emphasis placed on the number 7. Their position triggered various revolts against the ruling caliph.

The Mu'tazilites: Union of Theology and Reason

The vigorous Mu'tazilite sect appeared in Syria and Iraq during the Ummayyad caliphate. Composed largely of converts who were familiar with Jewish, Christian, Greek, and Zoroastrian thought, their purpose, according to Noss and Noss (1994:609), was apparently to convince non-Muslims of the validity of the Muslim faith. They were the Islamic equivalent to the Christian apologists who had preceded them.

The Mu'tazilites emphasized the free response of the individual to moral demands prescribed in the Qur'an. Not only does Allah "challenge the conscience of individuals, he also seeks their rational assent" (ibid.). They also proclaimed the "heretical idea" that Allah is a god of grace and not a pre-destinator of human souls. "How could it be just for God to predestinate a person to commit moral sin or to maintain an attitude of heresy or unbelief, and then punish that person for being guilty of either? It would not be fair or right" (ibid.)

The greatest dissension caused by the Mu'tazilites was their denial that the Qur'an was eternal and uncreated, precisely against the position held by most Muslims. They argued that for it to be eternal, it would have existed co-eternally with Allah, which to them amounted to polytheism. They also held that God was Spirit and not flesh-and-blood, which latter doctrine many Muslims had come to believe. This movement was finally crushed in the 10th century, but not before it had greatly influenced Islamic thought and learning.

Bridging Two Worlds

The Drawing Table

1. Describe the problems caused by Muhammad's not naming a successor.
2. Why were Jews and Christians tolerated in the early history of Islam?
3. Why did Islam turn to worldwide military conquest?
4. How do the Shiites view other Muslims?
5. What denial by the Mu'tazilites caused the greatest dissension in Islam?

Bridge-Building Tools

William J. Saal, on pages 162-164 in *Reaching Muslims for Christ*, suggests using Luke's Gospel in nine sections with Muslims. If you do not have access to his book, write your own evangelistic sessions based on a study of Luke. You might choose to use John or one of the other Gospel accounts highlighting a gradual revelation of who Jesus really is. Pray for opportunities to share in a Bible study with a Muslim friend.

Jesus Begins His Ministry and Claims Messiahship

As soon as Jesus was baptized, he went up out of the water. At that moment heaven was opened, and he saw the Spirit of God descending like a dove and lighting on him. And a voice from heaven said, "This is my Son, whom I love; with him I am well pleased" (*Matthew 3:16-17*).

"For God so loved the world that he gave his one and only Son, that whoever believes in him shall not perish but have eternal life. For God did not send his Son into the world to condemn the world, but to save the world through him. Whoever believes in him is not condemned, but whoever does not believe stands condemned already because he has not believed in the name of God's one and only Son" (*John 3:16-18*).

"But do not think I will accuse you before the Father. Your accuser is Moses, on whom your hopes are set. If you believed Moses, you would believe me, for he wrote about me. But since you do not believe what he wrote, how are you going to believe what I say?" (*John 5:45-47*).

"No one can come to me unless the Father who sent me draws him, and I will raise him up at the last day. It is written in the Prophets: 'They will all be taught by God.' Everyone who listens to the Father and learns from him comes to me. No one has seen the Father except the one who is from God; only he has seen the Father. I tell you the truth, he who believes has everlasting life. I am the bread of life . . . . This bread is my flesh, which I will give for the life of the world" (*John 6:44-51*).

Jesus replied, "If I glorify myself, my glory means nothing. My Father, whom you claim as your God, is the one who glorifies me. Though you do not know him, I know him . . . . Your father Abraham rejoiced at the thought of seeing my day; he saw it and was glad." "You are not yet fifty years old," the Jews said to him, "and you have seen Abraham!" "I tell you the truth," Jesus answered, "before Abraham was born, I am!" (*John 8:54-58*).

5

The Classical Period of Islamic Development

When 'Ali was assassinated in AD 661, the Umayyad family was able to gain control of the caliphate, moving it to Damascus. The Umayyad Dynasty continued in power for a century. However, it was more like a kingdom than a religion, with the caliphs ruling in absolute power and luxury.

In 750 the Abbasids, a group of non-Arab Muslims, joined forces with the Shiites and routed the Umayyads. They then moved the capital to a new "city of peace" on the Tigris River, Baghdad. They named a descendent of Muhammad as caliph, with him and his successors ruling as oriental kings in what is called the Golden Age of Islam. They attracted poets, artists, and philosophers. They enjoyed large harems, travel, wealth, and luxury under such caliphs as Huran al-Rashid. From this period came the stories of the Arabian Nights. As Ludwig says, "Baghdad society here seems a world away from the Arabic culture of the Qur'an" (Ludwig 1966:458).

The greatest contribution of this period was to scholarship. Muslim scholars translated works of Plato and Aristotle, and turned to questions of reason, revelation, divine power, and human will. Medicine, astronomy, mathematics, architecture, art, and many other disciplines flourished, well ahead of anything that Europe had to offer in that period. Scholars such as Avicenna, al-Ghazali, and Averroes came to prominence. Some Muslim scholars, such as Averroes, even attempted to bring about a synthesis of Judaism, Christianity, Islam, and other faiths.

Rival Islamic Spheres of Influence

The Abbasids were not the only Islamic rulers at the time. In Spain the capital city of Cordova flourished under a rival caliphate of the Umayyad family. In Egypt a powerful group developed under a Shiite dynasty called the Fatimid (after Fatima, Muhammad's daughter). The Fatimids built Cairo and founded an important university.

The Classical age of Islam ended in the 11th and 12th centuries, when Turkish tribes conquered Iran and Iraq, assuming power over them. The new Turkish sovereign, called the Prince of Princes, ruled Islam, placing the caliph in a figurehead position only.

Turkish and Mongol Rise to Power

The Seljuk Turks dominated Islam by the 11th century, capturing Jerusalem and cutting off Christian pilgrims' access to the Holy City. This precipitated the Crusades, with European forces recapturing Jerusalem in 1099 (Latourette 1975:409-410). Jerusalem remained in European hands for less than a century and was then recaptured by the Seljuk leader Saladin in 1187.

When the Mongols rose to power in the 13th century, Islamic power waned. The Mongol hordes captured and burned Baghdad in 1258, leaving the Muslim world in disarray.

The Rise of Sufism

Some Islamic scholars and religious leaders, abhorring the opulence of the Baghdad court, turned to mysticism, which clashed with orthodox beliefs. These heretics were called *Sufis* and their movement, *Sufism*.

Muhammad and the early caliphs had lived a frugal lifestyle, with 'Ali impoverishing himself to aid the destitute. The Sufis attempted to imitate their style, denouncing the amenities of the court. They received their name from the Arabic word, *suf* (wool), but were also called *faquirs* (poor ones).

Sufis emphasized the inner qualities of love and con-templation over the outward fulfillment of legal requirements in religion. They followed the outer path, the *shari'ah*, to Allah, "in order to break attachment to earthly things. But at its higher levels the *Tariqa* (the inner way) became a way of . . . meditation, leading finally to freedom from attachment to self and a 'passing away' (*fara*) into God" (Ludwig 1996: 462).

Clashes with orthodox views soon set in. Some Sufis felt that they had arisen above the Shari'ah and therefore could willfully ignore and even violate the law. Others sought communion with God at all costs. One Sufi mystic, al-Hallaj, even described his deep union with God as "I am the Truth, e.g., God."

The Sufi sect finally came to be acceptable to mainline orthodoxy. It has existed as a legitimate mystical element in Islam since about the year 1000 and is considered today to be the "heartbeat of Islam."

This movement itself eventually fragmented, with one line called the *Dervish Orders*. The Dervishes (*darwish*, the Persian word for poor) practiced poverty as a way of life. They also practiced ecstatic experience and tongue-speaking, which attracted many people to them out of curiosity. The more extreme Dervishes act in the role of *shamans* (witch doctors or medicine men), swallowing or walking across live coals, passing needles, hooks, and knives through their bodies and engaging in other esoteric practices, including veneration of their saints in the Roman Catholic style.

Medieval Islamic Empires

Following the devastation wreaked by the Mongols, new Muslim empires arose: the Safavid in Iran, the Mogul in India, and the Ottoman, centered in western Asia.

In Iran Muslim leaders followed the Shiite tradition. The *shahs* (political leaders) who established the Safavid Dynasty (1502-1736) claimed decent from the seventh imam and thus were entitled to be the true heirs of Muhammad. Under the leadership of Shah 'Abbas, they built the cultural center of Isfahan, which attracted both travelers and Muslim scholars.

In the 10th century Muslim warriors invaded India, battling against the polytheism encountered there. Then in the early 1500s an army led by Babur, a descendant of Genghis Khan, founded the Mogul Empire in northern India. The ruler Akbar, grandson of Babur, was a Muslim, although he granted religious freedom and discussion, even in the royal palace. The legacy of the Mogul Empire encompasses the largest segment of Muslims in the world today. It is scattered in India, Pakistan, Bangladesh, Malaysia, and Indonesia.

The Ottoman Empire dates from the early 1300s and was founded in Asia Minor by the Turk Osman. The Ottomans soon subjugated much of the Muslim world, became guardians of the Islamic holy sites and claimed to be the true protectors of Islam.

The Ottomans conquered Constantinople, the Balkans, and most of Hungary, and crushed a Turkish uprising. Although the Ottoman Empire reached its zenith under Süleyman I the Magnificent (1520-1566), Islam became under his leadership only a religious bureaucracy within the political system.

A long period of stagnation and decline began after the Mongol invasion and continued during the period of these three empires. Ludwig says that the Renaissance, the Scientific Revolution, and the Enlightenment enveloping the West did not penetrate Muslim society until at least the 19th century (1966:465). Modernity has invaded Islam only in this century and has still not reached the entire Muslim world. Some regions, such as Afghanistan until the current war, are repressively anti-modern.

More Recent Developments in Islam

This brings us to more recent times in the history of Islam. Western cultural influences have made inroads into some Islamic regions, especially those farthest-removed from Mecca in distance. Affluence in the Arabian Peninsula countries has made inroads into traditional Islamic thought and practice.

The Classical Period of Islamic Development

Secularism has been a result of these outside influences in some countries. Young Turks, overthrowing the Ottoman Empire in 1924, brought about changes that were intended to modernize and secularize Turkey. As a result Turkey may be the most secular and open of the Islamic nations. Leftist groups in Algeria, Albania, Libya, Syria, Egypt, and other countries have brought about a softening of Islamic traditionalism and a more accepting attitude toward western modernity. This has caused a violent reaction from fundamentalists in these countries. The result has been an attempt to re-introduce traditional Islamic dress and practice, in some cases successful and in others not.

Examples of this upheaval may be found periodically in such countries as Sudan, Egypt, Syria, Iraq, Iran, and Afghanistan. Shah Muhammad Pahlavi of Iran fled political chaos in 1979, opening the door for the return of the exiled Ayatollah Khomeini. He, in turn, "proceeded with his plans for revitalizing Islamic traditions. He demanded that women return to the veil . . . banned alcohol and mixed bathing, and prohibited music from all radio and television programs" (*Information Please Almanac* 1995:206). In Lagos, Nigeria, the government, dominated politically by Muslims, constructed a national mosque of magnificent design. Christian forces, however, objected, succeeding in receiving government approval for a national cathedral adjacent to the national mosque.

Western cultural influences continue in Islamic lands, as western industries, banks, television, and other signs of westernization flood them. Incidentally, this is the very thing that fundamentalist Muslims fear and react against violently at times. "New concepts of law and political organization, new forms of commercial and industrial enterprise, new modes of transport . . . improvement in agriculture, medicine and never-before-dreamed-of wealth through the exploitation of newly-discovered natural resources" (Noss and Noss 1994: 634) have brought immense change to such nations as Saudi Arabia, Kuwait, and the United Arab Emirates.

Islam in countries farther removed from the center have

adapted the religion to their own cultural situation. Thus, Islam as it is viewed in Indonesia, Malaysia, India, and China is different in some respects from that practiced in Saudi Arabia.

In Indonesia, for instance, "much of Islam had been filtered through a pantheistic, mystical Indian culture before its arrival" (Noss and Noss 1994:644). Added to this was its superimposition on a cultural and religious base of long standing, Hinduism. Islam was seen as a means of freeing oneself from Hindu oppression. It offered an alternative way to both political and religious freedom. Today, there is much diversification in Indonesian Islam. Distinctions are made between the truly devout Muslims (*santri*) and the masses (*abangan*), the latter syncretizing Muslim practices with those of their former faiths.

Not only have there been modernizing movements in Islam, there have also been "prophetical" returns to fundamentalism. One such as the *Wahhabi Reform Movement*. In an attempt to purify Islam of the traditions, beliefs, and practices it had acquired over the centuries and in a variety of cultures, Muhammad ibn 'Abd al-Wahhab called for a return to the Qur'an and the Sunnah. His followers destroyed tombs and shrines dedicated to saints, initiated a new level of religious education and enforced Islamic morality (Ludwig 1996:467). They eventually gained control of Mecca and imposed their policies in Arabia. These still hold sway in that country, the most fundamental and traditional of all of the Islamic countries.

A different kind of reformation was that of the *Ahmadiya*. In the closing decades of the 1800s, Mirza Ghulam Ahmad received homage as a Mahdi. Reading the Bible, he concluded that he was the returned Messiah. Finally, he proclaimed himself an *avatar* (reincarnation) of the Hindu god, Krishna. Yet, he held himself to be a perfect Muslim, in that he was Muhammad, who had reappeared. His followers have split into several branches, but most of them consider him to have been a genuine renewer of the Faith.

Although Ahmadiya's roots go back beyond 1844, in that year Mirza named himself Bab-ud-Din (Gate of the Faith). He taught that his mission was to prepare the way for a prophet even greater than he and classified his "scriptures" as equal to, if not superior to, the Qur'an.

He was executed in 1850, but one of his disciples, a young man who took the name, Baha'u'llah (Glory of God), announced that he was the one of whom the Bab had prophesied. He called upon all religions to unite under him, since "every religion contains some truth, because all prophets are witnesses to the one Truth that Bahaism supremely represents" (Noss and Noss 1994:649-650).

Contemporary Islamic Movements

In 1928 the Muslim Brotherhood, a mixed spiritual-social-political fundamentalist movement, began in Egypt. It was rooted in the idea of using violence to achieve the ideal Islamic state.

> The Brotherhood aims at imposing its concept of law and its standards of behavior on the whole community, by persuasion and example, if possible, by force if not. To the Brothers, religion and politics are inseparable, and any Muslim society failing to live by the Koran and Sharia is impious . . . . When preaching, good works, education and exhortation failed to cleanse society to their satisfaction, the Brothers resorted to terrorism and assassination (Lippman 1990:157).

The Brotherhood is still alive and active in fomenting insurrection and terrorism. To its thinking, no secular laws, no civil state, and no politics can be permitted. All states must be theocratic, serving only Allah and living only by the Qur'an.

Another Egyptian-based fundamentalist group dedicated to terrorism is Islamic Jihad. It was responsible for the assassination of Egyptian President Anwar Sadat as punishment for his signing a peace treaty with Israel.

Hezbollah (Party of God) is a contemporary radical movement operating primarily in Lebanon and backed by Iraq and Syria. Hezbollah is "a militant Islamic organization that is waging a guerrilla war against Israel . . . . " (*National Geographic*, September 1997:119).

In Israel, itself, the Palestinians have formed a related group called Hamas. Like Hezbollah, it is dedicated to the overthrow of Israel by fair means or foul and retaking all of Palestine. Its frequent terrorist attacks against Israelis indicate its mentality.

More recently al-Qaeda (or al-Qaida), the terrorist movement led and financed by Osama bin Laden, is making the news daily. It appears certain that al-Qaeda is behind bombings of the World Trade Center, U.S. embassies in Kenya and Tanzania, and the U.S.S. Cole, as well as the destruction of the Trade Center towers and the Pentagon September 11, 2001. Osama bin Laden called for the utter destruction of the U.S. and praised his terrorists for their total submission to Allah in their suicidal mission.

There are many other associated terrorist groups and cells. All of these are connected in some way with Islam and have as their goal the destruction of the U.S. and its allies, free-market economies, democracy, materialism, secularism, Western cultures, and all religions not Islamic.

The Black Muslim Movement

In the United States the Black Muslim sect, or the Lost-Found Nation of Islam, began to flourish beginning in 1930. It was founded by W.D. Fard (Master Wali Farrad Muhammad) as a means of redeeming American blacks by giving them identity and pride through Islam, as he inter-preted it for American consumption. He referred to himself as Allah Incarnate and his successor, Elijah Poole (Elijah Muhammad) as the Messenger of Allah. He then disappeared and Poole became the sole leader.

This movement's theology was "that 'so-called Negroes' were descendants of a black Original Man and had been

Muslims from the very ancient tribe of Shabazz, long before Muhammad. Yakut, a mad scientist, rebelled against Allah and created the weak and hybrid white race of devils, who are responsible for the temporary degradation of blacks, but in a final Armageddon Allah will overthrow evil" (Noss and Noss 1994:650).

Poole insisted on a strong work ethic, abstinence, building self-esteem through cooperative efforts, refusing all participation in politics, and initiating no violence. He also promoted education, business ventures for blacks, and highly-trained black youth.

Malcolm Little, better known as Malcolm X or Malik Shabazz, broke with Elijah in 1963. He formed his own Muslim Mosque Inc. in 1964, but his leadership was short-lived. He was assassinated in 1965.

Elijah Poole was succeeded by his son Wallace in 1975. Wallace led the movement in the direction of Sunni orthodoxy. He encouraged participation in politics and military service.

In 1978 Louis Farrakhan, a disciple of the early Malcolm X, challenged Wallace, calling for the re-establishment of Malcolm's Nation of Islam and his original teaching. Farrakhan is best known for his fiery oratory and his organization of the Million-Man March to Washington, D.C. One of his more famous disciples is the boxing champion Muhammad Ali. When asked by Howard Bingham, author of *Muhammad Ali: A Thirty-Year Journey* and one of Ali's closest confidants since 1962, "What does your faith mean to you?"

[It] means [a] ticket to heaven. One day we're all going to die, and God's going to judge us, [our] good and bad deeds. [If the] bad outweighs the good, you go to hell; if the good outweighs the bad, you go to heaven.

[I'm] thinking about the judgment day and how you treat people wherever you go. Help somebody through charity, because when you do, it's been recorded (*Reader's Digest*, December 2001, p. 93).

For a time it was popular for black athletes to join the Black Muslim movement and to take on Arab names. In more recent years this trend has seemed to diminish.

A Common Doctrinal and Traditional Thread

Noss and Noss say, "Islam is not and never has been a monolithic faith. Divergences in doctrine, divisions of a political nature, and variations in law and the development of the spiritual life have frequently occurred" (Noss and Noss 1994: 619).

Talmadge adds to this point: " . . . the Muslim world is no monolith . . . there is great diversity among Muslim countries in different regions . . . . In countries across the world [Islam] has been adopted in strikingly different ways" (Talmadge, Associated Press release, October 12, 2001).

Talmadge believes, I think correctly, that "Mecca and the Middle East will always be at the heart of Islam. Asia may be where its future will be shaped" (ibid.). He bases this on the fact that the demographic center of the Islamic world is in Pakistan, India, Bangladesh, Malaysia, and Indonesia, far removed in distance and culture.

Yet, despite all of the divisions and sects found in Islam, and despite all of the cultural differences that exist, there are *common threads* throughout this diverse faith. 1) The core of these threads is the Qur'an, which is reverenced by all elements in Islam. 2) Muhammad is a second vital strand in the faith of these diverse groups. 3) Another strand is a common tongue, Arabic, among many Muslims. 4) And Muslims share a common cultural heritage in a large region at Islam's historical core.

Bridging Two Worlds

The Drawing Table

1. What impact did scholarship have on Islam's Golden Age?
2. Why do you suppose modernity has not reached the entire Muslim world?
3. Explain the reason some Islamic countries revert to fundamentalism in response to threatening westernization.
4. Explain why the terrorist's common goal is destruction.
5. What are some common threads in the contemporary Islamic world?

Bridge-Building Tools

Go to the local library, college, or the Internet to learn of the contributions of Islamic artists, scientists, and other scholars. Use these examples with a Muslim friend to begin conversations. Pray for opportunities to share the gospel with your friend.

Research modern Islamic sects around the world and list their differences. Discover which countries might be more receptive to the gospel based on their potential openness to learning. Write to missionaries in those countries and ask how you can help them.

Jesus Claims to Be God's Son and the Resurrection

Jesus said to her, "I am the resurrection and the life. He who believes in me will live, even though he dies; and whoever lives and believes in me will never die. Do you believe this?" (*John 11:25-26*).

"If you are the Christ, " they said, "tell us." Jesus answered, "If I tell you, you will not believe me, and if I asked you, you would not answer. But from now on, the Son of Man will be seated at the right hand of the mighty God." They all asked, "Are you then the Son of God?" He replied, "You are right in saying I am" (*Luke 22:67-70*).

Pilate had a notice prepared and fastened to the cross. It read: JESUS OF NAZARETH, THE KING OF THE JEWS. Many of the Jews read this sign, for the place where Jesus was crucified was near the city, and the sign was written in Aramaic, Latin and Greek. The chief priests of the Jews protested to Pilate, "Do not write 'The King of the Jews,' but that this man claimed to be king of the Jews." Pilate answered, "What I have written, I have written" (*John 19:19-22*).

He said to them, "How foolish you are, and how slow of heart to believe all that the prophets have spoken! Did not the Christ have to suffer these things and then enter his glory?" And beginning with Moses and all the Prophets, he explained to them what was said in all the Scriptures concerning himself (*Luke 24:25-27*).

Then Jesus came to them and said, "All authority in heaven and on earth has been given to me. Therefore go and make disciples of all nations, baptizing them in the name of the Father and of the Son and of the Holy Spirit, and teaching them to obey everything I have commanded you. And surely I am with you always, to the very end of the age" (*Matthew 28:18-20*).

6

Basic Muslim Beliefs

In any religious system there are basic beliefs that hold faith together, despite its differences with other religions. Islam is no exception. Its foundational beliefs are held by most Muslims worldwide. Among these are the well-known Pillars of the Faith, but there are a number of others as well. Let us begin with the Pillars:

The Five Pillars of the Islamic Faith

On top of the Qur'an were erected five basic practices, or pillars. These are confession, prayer, almsgiving, fasting, and pilgrimage.

• **Confession, or** *Shahadah,* is basic to Islamic faith. In Arabic it is *Ilaha'illa Allah. Muhammad rasul Allah.* Translated, this is "I testify that there is no God but God; I testify that Muhammad is the Messenger of God." This confession "is a public witnessing to the unity of God and to the Qur'an as God's final revelation" (Ludwig 1996:484). To this explanation must be added that Muhammad, along with Allah, is always on the lips of Muslims as they chant this confession at least five times a day. It is also used in a visual form on walls, ceilings, posters, banners, curtains, and other materials. In Kenya I saw it lettered on a large truck.

• **Prayer, or** *Salat,* is the heart and soul of Muslim life. Prayer is a public expression of praise and submission to Allah. This is done at set hours worldwide five times a day— early morning, noon, mid-afternoon, sunset, and evening. All Muslims are expected to cease what they are doing and to face Mecca, going through the ritual of standing, kneeling, bowing, and falling prostrate. (Obviously in today's world not everyone can stop to go through this formula. Muslim airline pilots in flight would be a good example of this.) It is a highly standardized formula in which only Arabic, the "sacred tongue" can be used. At the Friday noon hour Muslims are expected to assemble at a local mosque as a congregation. The imam or other leader guides the group in prayer and also preaches a sermon or gives an exhortation.

• **Almsgiving,** *Zakah* **or** *Zakat,* is the religious duty of all Muslims to share a percentage of their income and goods with those who have little. " … all wealth belongs to God, who has directed us to share it with those [Muslims] who are less fortunate, as a sign that all are equal before God and deserve a just and fair livelihood" (Ludwig 1996:486). This is more than just charity. It is a form of required religious tax exacted on all Muslims and on all forms of their wealth.

• **Fasting, or** *Sawm.* The month of Ramadan was designated by Muhammad as a month of fasting, in which all Muslims were to abstain from food from sunup to sunset throughout that month. This is considered a sacred duty in the ninth month of the Islamic calendar—in honor of the revelation of the Qur'an. To Muslims, fasting is not a means of punishing the body, but of regaining dominance over it and of learning self-control and brotherhood.

• **The Pilgrimage, or** *Hajj.* A pilgrimage to Mecca is required of all Muslims who are physically able at least once in their lifetime. They cannot borrow money for this journey, nor deprive their family to take it. They must save, often for many years, for this trek. They must also dress in white and vow to abstain from sex, haircuts, jewelry, arguments, and violence. Ludwig notes about the Hajj: "The Pilgrimage epitomized the ritual duty of Muslims. It is a dramatic connection to the sacred story, walking in the footsteps of Abraham, Hagar, Ishmael and Muhammad. It is an intensely individual spiritual experience, and at the same time, a moving communal experience" (ibid.).

The Hajj includes various required activities, many of which had been practiced in pre-Islamic Arabia. For instance, the first ritual is walking and/or trotting around the Ka'bah seven times in a counterclockwise direction. Pilgrims reach out to touch or kiss the sacred Black Stone, located in a corner of the Ka'bah. It is interesting to observe that, although Islam abhors all idolatry, Muslims' reverence for the stone, by any definition, is idolatrous.

The pilgrim also runs to the sacred well of Zamzam, where tradition says that Hagar and Ishmael were saved from dying of thirst by Allah's providing this well for them. Arriving there, the pilgrim thankfully drinks from the well.

On the eighth day of the Pilgrimage all participants move out into the desert, where they live in tents for several days. On the ninth day there is a special ritual called *wuquf*, in which all pilgrims stand from noon until sunset, praising Allah.

Final rituals including Stoning and the Feast of Sacrifice, or *'id al-adha*. Tradition says that Abraham brought Ishmael to this desert to sacrifice him. Satan attempted to intervene, but Ishmael stoned him. Pilgrims re-enact this by throwing 49 stones at three stone "Satans." Then all pilgrims (and their fellow Muslims worldwide) ritually kill an animal and feast with their families (an echo of the Jewish Passover feast. Then they return to Mecca for more circlings of the Ka'bah before going home.

The greatest honor a Muslim can have is to make the Pilgrimage. Those men who have done so are qualified to wear the white cap signifying their having participated in the Pilgrimage.

• Some would add **Holy War or Jihad** as a sixth pillar. According to Islamic teaching, Jihad is struggle—inner struggle, called the Greater Jihad, and struggle against all infidels and enemies, called the Lesser Jihad. When calls are made by Osama bin Laden, by Afghan leaders, or by Khomeini, they mean holy war against the infidels worldwide. Bloodshed, in the name of Allah and for his cause, is justifiable in the name of Jihad. Abu Bakr, Muhammad's immediate successor as leader of the Muslim movement, told his followers, "And I would have you know that fighting for religion is an act of obedience to Allah" (cited in Sumrall 1981:95). His modern successors believe this, with the more fundamentalist and radical of them enforcing it by rhetoric and armed conflict. To them, the crux of the matter is religious, not political or economic. It is a struggle between the faith (Islam) and the infidels. According to Esposito, Jihad is "the obligation incumbent on all Muslims, as individuals and as a community, to exert themselves to realize God's will, to lead a virtuous life and to extend the Islamic community . . . . " (Esposito 1988:95).

A related meaning is the struggle for or in defense of the faith. Although jihad is not meant necessarily to include armed warfare, it has always implied such violence, as practiced by Muhammad and the caliphs following him. In recent years Mamaat al-Jihad (Islamic Jihad) assassinated President Anwar Sadat of Egypt because of his having made a peace accord with Israel. In 1997 muazzins (or muezzins) atop their minarets in some cities of Pakistan announced that the time had arrived for jihad against the Christians. When the resulting rioting was over, hundreds of people, a thousand homes, 13 church buildings, a medical dispensary, and a school had been destroyed (news bulletins from Pakistan sent to *The Christian Chronicle*, Oklahoma City, Oklahoma, in July 1997).

Other Holy Days and Observances

Muslims also observe various other special days and practices. These include the Feast of Fast-breaking, or 'id al-fitr, which comes on the day following the Fast of Ramadan.

Another special festival is in honor of Muhammad's birth, on the 12th day of the third month, and in honor of the Hijra from Mecca to Medina, which marks the beginning of the Muslim year.

Rituals observing passages of life, although not mentioned in the Qur'an, are important to Muslims. For example, right after birth the call to prayer and the summons to perform the prayer ritual are whispered in a Muslim baby's left and right ears. Sacrifices are performed on the seventh day after birth. Circumcision is practiced on all male babies on the eighth day, just as in Judaism. In the case of Indonesia, circumcision is practiced when a boy reaches 12 years of age, as a sign of his passing to Muslim manhood. On the 40th day after the birth of a child, the mother is purified in a duplication of the Hebrew purification rite.

Marriage is not observed as a sacrament, but there are many traditional rituals connected with it. Death is also an important ritual period. The Islamic writer, al-Ghazali, gave this advice about death: "When you want to go to sleep, lay out your bed pointing to Mecca, and sleep on your right side . . . . Remember that in like manner you will lie in the tomb . . . only your works will be with you, only the effort you have made will be rewarded" (Watt 1953:115).

Other Muslim Beliefs

What do Muslims believe? Interestingly, in a wide variety of matters and manners. There is first "official belief" as prescribed in the Qur'an. Then there is "modified belief" as incorporated in the Ahadith. There is a also a body of beliefs developed by consensus of Islamic leaders, by analogy, Islamic law and particular points of doctrine and behavior developed by the different Islamic sects. Finally, there is "folk belief," which goes far beyond any official source, relying instead on tradition and legend.

Official Beliefs

Officially, all Muslims are expected to believe in:
• One God, Allah, with no other beings associated with Him except angels.
• One holy book, the Qur'an, which, as we have pointed-ed out, is asserted to have been revealed to Muhammad, and him alone, over a period of time by the Angel Gabriel. This book is said to be the final revelation of Allah, replacing the Old and New Testaments. Some Muslims believe that it has always existed, while others believe that it was created by Allah as a divine miracle and is thus inferior to Him (Geisler and Saleeb 1993:180). Whichever of the two is more correct in Muslim eyes, it is still considered perfect in every detail.

• Muhammad is the final and greatest prophet of Allah, as promised to Moses in Deuteronomy 18:17-19. No other prophet is ever expected.

• All Muslims must rigorously observe the Five Pillars of the Faith.

• Jihad is to be zealously practiced.

• Muslims must abstain from pork and all alcoholic beverages. However, no such prohibition exists against tobacco and even stronger addictive drugs. Some Islamic countries grow and sell tobacco, while others grow poppies and sell their end product, heroin.

• Family law, which Esposito says, is the core of Islam's social structure (ibid.). This, along with polygamy, women's status, divorce, community, and related points, will be considered in Chapter 8.

• Punishment is required for adultery; thievery; blasphemy against Allah, the Qur'an, and Muhammad; unfaithfulness in observing any of the Five Pillars; and murder of a fellow Muslim. Traditionally, adultery required the execution of both guilty parties. Thievery was punished by having a hand of the culprit cut off. Blasphemy was punishable by death, as was murder of another Muslim. (How, then, was the killing of many Muslims in the World Trade Towers in Manhattan justified? By the principle, not found in the Qur'an, of collateral damage? Perhaps by the philosophy that the end justifies the means?) Unfaithfulness to Islam resulted in expulsion from the Faith. Turning to another religion or proselytizing another Muslim to Christianity was punishable by death. Killing a non-Muslim, and especially one considered a pagan, is considered to be no crime, but rather, a blessing for the one committing the act. A pro-Taliban youth put it this way: "The Americans love Coca Cola, but we love death" (reported in the media early in October 2001).

• A final Judgment, Heaven and Hell. Allah will judge all humans, but will give special honor to faithful Muslims, placing them in a physical Paradise in which they will enjoy all kinds of delicacies and be served by beautiful virgins. Non-Muslims will be consigned to Hell, along with all Muslims who have abandoned the Faith, blasphemed, or committed some other major crime against Allah and the Muslim community.

• Moral expediency, retaliation, and mercilessness, along with lying and deceiving, if they are intended to advance the cause of Islam. This is much like the Roman Catholic doctrine of mental reservation. Muhammad sanctioned raids on trading caravans, with him leading three of them. He approved of lying, if it would achieve his ends. He retaliated against his enemies or supposed enemies, showing no mercy to those who opposed him. He even said, "Allah wants no prisoners of war." (See Geisler and Saleeb 1993: 173-177 for more details on these points.)

The affirmation is often made that Islam is a peaceful religion. Not according to many passages in the Qur'an, nor according to Islam's history. The Qur'an says:

"Kill them (all opponents of Muhammad) wherever you find them, and drive them out from wherever they drove you out . . . ." (Sûrah 2:191).

"I will instill terror into the hearts of the unbelievers, smite ye above their necks and smite all their fingertips off them. It is not ye who slew them; it was God" (Sûrah 8:13-17).

"Fight and slay the pagans wherever ye find them and seize them, beleaguer them, and lie in wait for them, in every stratagem . . . ." (Sûrah 9:5).

"Fight those who do not believe in God and the last day . . . and fight People of the Book (Christians and Jews) who do not accept the religion of truth (Islam) until they pay tribute by hand, being inferior" (Sûrah 9.29).

. . . "slay the idolaters wherever ye find them" (Sûrah 9:5).

Hear further what the Qur'an says about warfare against non-Muslims:

"Fight against such of those who have been given the Scripture as believe not in Allah . . . ."(Sûrah 9:20).

The Qur'an is filled, says Chavez, with "elaborate instructions on the conduct of war, the methods of executing the infidels, the rewards that will accrue to those martyred in a holy war" (Chavez column in *The Daily Oklahoman*, October 10, 2001). In a televised statement October 9, 2001, a leading spokesman for al-Qaida said, "young Muslims are just as eager to die [for their cause] as Americans are to live." Those who claim that Islam is a religion of peace do not know the Qur'an well, nor do they know the history of Islam. Neither Islam nor Christianity can claim to have had a peaceful past.

As for Islamic history, Islam has always been intent on world domination. Into the 16th century its expansion was primarily by armed might, except for some people groups who, seeing the power of the Islamic tide, embraced it for self-preservation or for political reasons. Such Islamic rulers as Saladin and Süleyman I were brilliant and single-minded military leaders.

But does Islam still desire to dominate the world by any means possible? According to Ashurst, "Islam is intent on world domination, religiously and politically, using whatever methods may be considered the most expedient . . . ." (Ashurst and Masood 1994:11). Islamic fundamentalists and terrorists are merely pushing their doctrine to its logical end.

Traditional and Folk Beliefs

In addition to the basic rules by which Islam has functioned, there are many other traditional and folk beliefs in the Islamic world. One of these is that Muhammad was transported miraculously to Jerusalem on a divinely provided mount, where he ascended to Heaven for further revelations from Allah. This belief is justified by a passage from the Qur'an: "Glorified be He Who carried His servant by night from the Inviolable Place of Worship to the Far Distant Place of Worship the neighbourhood whereof We have blessed, that We might show him of Our tokens. Lo! He, only He, is the Hearer, the Seer" (Sûrah 17:1).

Many traditions center on Muhammad, himself. One is that at his birth Gabriel cut open Muhammad's breast, removed and cleansed his heart, filling it with wisdom (Geisler and Saleeb 1988:161). Allah was supposed to have sent 3,000 angels to protect Muhammad, giving him victory in the Battle of Badr against his Arabian adversaries. He is also said to have thrown a handful of dirt into his enemies' eyes, blinding them.

Muslim tradition attributes to Muhammad many other "miracles" not claimed, in all fairness, by him. One is essentially a duplication of Christ's miraculous feeding of the 5,000 (Matthew 14:13-21). Others have him saluted by trees and mountains, his turning a tree branch into a sword, providing water for his 10,000 troops, splitting the moon in half, turning water into milk and cursing an enemy, who sank with his horse into solid ground (Geisler and Saleeb 1988:158-164).

Muhammad is held in such high regard that he is thought to have never sinned, despite the fact that he is told in the Qur'an to ask forgiveness for his sins (Sûrahs 40:55 and 41:19). Even in a strictly monotheistic faith he has been elevated to a level above that of Christ. He is given power to intercede for other human beings. So the Urdu poet, Mir Taqi Mir, writes: "Why do you worry, O Mir, thinking of your black book? The person of the Seal of the Prophets is a guarantee of your salvation" (Schimmel 1985:88).

Muhammad is thought to have pre-existed the world and to have been the reason for the world's creation (ibid.:92). The Ahadith has Allah saying, "I am Ahmad without 'm'" (Gudel 1982:73). Ahmad is a synonym for Muhammad. Dropping the letter "m" turns the word into Ahad, a name for God. Muhammad is thought to have been the light from which God created the world. He is called the Savior of the World and the Lord of the Universe. One Muslim commentator is said to have declared, "You may curse Allah if you will, but you dare not disparage Muhammad" (source unconfirmed).

Bridging Two Worlds

The Drawing Table
1. Do Christians have anything like the five pillars of Islam? List any corresponding beliefs in Christianity.
2. How is jihad applied to a holy war against infidels?
3. Why would Islamic youth say, "Americans love Coca Cola, but we love death"?
4. Is Islam intent on world domination? Why or Why not?
5. Why would followers exaggerate claims for their leader? Can you name any exaggerations that Christians have claimed for Jesus?

Bridge-Building Tools
Since the first chapter, you may have been compiling a notebook with counterpoints to the Five Pillars of Islam. Add to your notebook what you have learned from your study of Islam and your Bible study. Set times to compare your notebook with those of other Christians so that you can share information and evangelistic strategies.

Learn of mission efforts to the Islamic world. Consult a Christian college for organizations or parachurch works that specialize in reaching Muslims. If you have the time and desire, volunteer to help an international Bible study program such as World Bible School, World English Institute, or International Bible School. You can correspond through Bible lessons with Muslim students around the world without leaving your home. (See "Resources" at the end of this book.)

Historical Proof of Jesus' Resurrection

After his suffering, he showed himself to these men and gave many convincing proofs that he was alive. He appeared to them over a period of forty days and spoke about the kingdom of God. On one occasion, while he was eating with them, he gave them this command: "Do not leave Jerusalem, but wait for the gift my Father promised, which you have heard me speak about. For John baptized with water, but in a few days you will be baptized with the Holy Spirit" . . . . After he said this, he was taken up before their very eyes, and a cloud hid him from their sight (*Acts 1:3-9*).

"You stiff-necked people, with uncircumcised hearts and ears! You are just like your fathers: You always resist the Holy Spirit! Was there ever a prophet your fathers did not persecute? They even killed those who predicted the coming of the Righteous One. And now you have betrayed and murdered him—you who have received the law that was put into effect through angels but have not obeyed it" . . . . Stephen, full of the Holy Spirit, looked up to heaven and saw the glory of God, and Jesus standing at the right hand of God. "Look," he said, "I see heaven open and the Son of Man standing at the right hand of God" (*Acts 7:51-56*).

This righteousness from God comes through faith in Jesus Christ to all who believe. There is no difference, for all have sinned and fall short of the glory of God, and are justified freely by his grace through the redemption that came by Christ Jesus (*Romans 3:22-24*).

For what I received I passed on to you as of first importance: that Christ died for our sins according to the Scriptures, that he was buried, that he was raised on the third day according to the Scriptures, and that he appeared to Peter, and then to the Twelve. After that, he appeared to more than five hundred of the brothers at the same time, most of whom are still living, though some have fallen asleep. Then he appeared to James, then to all the apostles, and last of all he appeared to me also, as to one abnormally born (*1 Corinthians 15:3-8*).

7

The Bible and the Qur'an

The Bible was originally called by Muslims *The Book*. It was also called in the Qur'an "the Book of God," "the Word of God," "a light and guidance to man," "a decision for all matters," "a guidance and mercy," "the illumination" and other such terms (Geisler and Saleeb 1993:207). Originally, Muhammad held it in high regard. The Qur'an tells Christians to investigate their own Scriptures to find God's will for them (Sûrah 5:50).

The Qur'an holds Jesus in the highest regard. In fact, He is given more space in it than anyone else, including Muhammad. But we will soon see what the present attitude is about Jesus.

Muslim Attitude toward the Bible

Yet, Muslims hasten to say that it has been superseded by the newer and final revelation, the Qur'an, something never mentioned in the Qur'anic text itself. Jeffery notes, "It is to be believed that the Qur'an is the noblest of the books . . . . It is the last of the God-given scriptures to come down, it abrogates all the books which preceded it . . . . It is impossible for it to suffer any change or alteration" (Jeffery 1958: 126-128).

Thus the Bible, although admittedly containing many spiritual truths, has been replaced—precisely the argument used by Joseph Smith for the *Book of Mormon*, by Charles T. Russell for his *New World Bible*, and by Ellen G. White, who claimed that it was necessary to encircle the Bible with her revelations. In addition, Muslims claim that the Bible has suffered extensive editing and changes, making it corrupted and therefore undependable as revelation. For evidence,

Muslim authorities point to the many different translations and versions of the Bible, all of which have some textual variations, while the Qur'an, in the Arabic, has suffered not one change since given. This is not totally true, as we have pointed out, initially there were variant versions and even the present Qur'an did not receive its final form until later.

Muslim Attitude toward Allah

To the Muslim Allah is everything. He is the creator of all things. He is described in the Qur'an as the Magnificent, the All-Knowing, the Sustainer, the Beneficent and many other descriptive words. Yet, he is different from Yahweh, the Supreme Father of the Bible.

As we have noted, Allah was one of more than 360 gods of ancient Arabia, but was the patron god of the Quraysh Tribe, that of Muhammad. Considered by that tribe, at least, as the paramount god, it became the chief guardian of that deity. "The cult of a deity termed simply, 'the god' (al-ilh) was known throughout southern Syria and northern Arabia in the days before Islam—Muhammad's father was named Abdullah (servant of Allah) where the building called the Kaorcbah was indisputably in his house" (*Oxford Encyclopedia of the Modern Islamic World*, Vol. 1:76-77).

Dr. Robert Morey writes:

Allah was the moon god; Muslims still use the crescent shape of the moon over their mosques. In Arabia, there was the female goddess who is the sun god, and a male one, the moon god. They got married and produced three goddesses who were called "the daughters of Allah." They are AL LAT, AL UZZA AND MANAT.

Muhammad's uncle's name was Abu Talib. These names reveal the personal devotion that Muhammad's pagan family had to the worship of Allah, the moon god (cited in *The Voice of the Martyrs*, November 2001:3).

This god, Allah, is markedly different from Yahweh. For instance, "Those [Christians and Jews] who incurred the curse of Allah and His wrath, those whom some He transformed into apes and swine . . . ." (Sûrah 9:5). Muhammad's god is absolutely demanding and unrelenting. In Sûrah 9:80 we read, ". . . though thou ask forgiveness for them seventy times Allah will not forgive them."

Muslim Attitude toward Christ

Isa al-Masih (Jesus) is clearly called in the Qur'an a prophet of Allah, superseded only by Muhammad (Sûrahs 4:171; 5:78). The words of Jesus, according to the Qur'an, are authentic. The Muslim scholar Muffasir declared, "Muslims believe all prophets to be truthful because they are commissioned in the service of the humanity by Almighty Allah" (Muffasir 1980:1). Here we see an obvious inconsistency. Since Christ called Himself the Son of God and a prophet of God cannot lie, then He is what He says He is:

"No one knows the Father except the Son" (Matthew 11:27).

"The Father loves the Son and has placed everything in his hands. Whoever believes in the Son has eternal life, but whoever rejects the Son will not see life, for God's wrath remains on him" (John 3:35-36).

"I and the Father are one" (John 10:30).

"He who hates me hates me hates my Father" (John 15:23).

Islam is therefore wrong in denying these words.

Although accepting Jesus' miraculous virgin birth, Muslims deny the real source of His existence and the purpose for His incarnation. They strongly deny that He could have been God, God's Son or God in the flesh, because that would make God divisible; that is, two Gods. Actually, Muhammad had the view that the Godhead or Trinity of Christianity was composed of God, Mary, and Jesus; that God had sexual relations with Mary and from this union produced Jesus (Sûrah 5:116; see also Kershaw 1978:10-11). Muhammad knew the Arabian religious tradition that Allah had many children, which he absolutely could not accept. With his rejection of this belief and the notion he had picked up from his view of the Christian faith of his century, it is little wonder than he rebelled against the whole idea of God having a physical or even divine Son. Muslims believe that God needs no help, as one of their leaders explained to me. He meant by this that God needs no Son. "Yet," I responded, "He uses angels. Are they not His helpers?" to this he didn't answer.

Muslims also deny that Jesus died on the cross and rose again, which is the heart of Christianity. They accept the fact of a crucifixion, but believe that, somehow, Judas Iscariot or another disciple was substituted for Christ, dying in His place on the cross. They cannot accept the fact that a great Prophet of God such as Jesus could ever be permitted to die ingloriously. It appeared to Muhammad that if God could not protect His prophet Jesus from a cruel death, then God must have failed, impossible for Muhammad to even consider (Anderson 1990:219). "And because of their saying, 'We slew the Messiah, Jesus Son of Mary, Allah's messenger—they slew him not nor crucified him, but it appeared so unto them . . . they slew him not for certain" (Sûrah 4:157).

The idea of a substitute prevails, especially in Sunni Islam. The apocryphal book, *The Gospel of Barnabas*, has been used by Muslims to back up the claim that Judas was really the one crucified. The Muslim jurist Baidawi has Jesus asking His disciples which one would take on His likeness, to be killed in His place and then go directly to Paradise. One accepted and thus the prophet Jesus was spared, to be able to eventually return to earth and kill the antichrist and all pigs, as well as breaking the cross, destroying all churches and synagogues, establishing Islam, living for 40 more years and then being buried beside Muhammad in Medina (Sox 1984:116-117).

In a tape by Ravi Zacharias, a noted Christian apologist, he argues as follows: The Qur'an claims that prophets are 100 percent reliable. Jesus claimed to be the final perfect revelation of God. Muhammad praised Christ as a great prophet. If Christ was wrong, then Muhammad was still wrong for falsely identifying Christ as a prophet (from an E-mail message to *The Christian Chronicle* in 1997).

Muslim Attitude toward the Holy Spirit

Muslims deny that there is such a being as the Holy Spirit. Allah is indivisible and there can be no other gods beside Him. Further, they insist that the Godhead, or Trinity, of the Christians is totally erroneous and a blasphemy, because this doctrine places other beings equal with or beside God.

The Bible, on the other hand, teaches that there is a Holy Spirit who has been in existence since before the creation. Genesis 1:2 says, "The Spirit of God moved on the face of the water." Revelation 1:17 affirms, at the very end of the Bible, that the Holy Spirit is alive and is involved in the invitation of Christ to turn to Him and be saved.

The Spirit was active throughout Old Testament times. Then, during the ministry of Christ, the Spirit descended on Him (Matthew 3:16-17; Luke 3:21-22; John 1:37). Note in these three passages that three divine manifestations or beings are involved—the Father (the voice from Heaven), the Spirit (descending in the form of a dove), and the Son, whom Heaven's voice declared to be God's Son.

These three are one, not three distinct gods, but one God in three manifestations. As we noted earlier, water exists in three forms, yet it is still water. The same is true for the Godhead. When Christ was on earth, He declared that He and the Father were one, yet He spoke to the Father and the Father to Him (John 10:30; 12:28). And He promised His followers the Holy Spirit, who would only come after He returned to Heaven (John 14:16-20; 16:7-11).

Muslim Attitude toward Sin

Islam affirms that sin consists primarily of failure to observe rigorously the Five Pillars of the Faith. Other sins include refusing to believe in Allah, practicing idolatry or polytheism, failing to believe in and follow the Qur'an, speaking evil of other Muslims, taking vengeance against them, lying to them, being insolent, drinking alcoholic beverages, eating pork, committing adultery or rape, and other kinds of moral misbehavior.

Murdering another Muslim is a cardinal sin, yet Muslims war against Muslims continually. Columnist Linda Chavez notes: "Some of the most brutal tactics of the fundamentalists have been used against fellow Muslims in Egypt, Morocco, Afghanistan and elsewhere" (an editorial in *The Daily Oklahoman*, October 10, 2001).

Muslim Attitude toward Non-believers

Murder of a non-believer is not considered a sin or a crime. Confiscating the goods of a non-believer, assassination, *jihad*, and other such acts against infidels are viewed as legitimate. Consider, for instance, Khomeini's issuance of a death warrant against Salman Rashdie, the English author who penned the book, *Satanic Verses*. Or the current call for jihad against all Americans.

Muslim Attitude toward Salvation

To Muslims, salvation consists of submission to Allah. Yet, there is no certainty of salvation from sin. According to Geisler and Saleeb (1993:126), from the very beginning of Islam "almost all Muslims have feared for their eternal destiny." When early Islamic leaders were asked if they were truly believers, their consistent answer was, "I hope so. If it be the will of Allah" (ibid.). Muhammad Ali, world celebrity boxer and dedicated Muslim, observed that, to him, his faith means a "ticket to heaven . . .God's going to judge us, good and bad deeds. [If the] bad outweighs the good, you go to hell. If the good outweighs the bad, you do to heaven" (*Reader's Digest*, December 2001:93). There remains the haunting question, "How can I know my good deeds have outweighed my bad deeds?"

The Bible teaches that sin consists of two basic aspects: those of commission (thoughts or acts contrary to the will of God as revealed in His Word) and those of omission (negligence in fulfilling the requirements that God has laid down for us (Matthew 23:23; Hebrews 10:26; 12:25). There are also degrees of sin, such as willful vs. ignorant (Numbers 15:28; Acts 3:17; 17:30). Sin is the transgression, public or private, of the law of God (1 John 3:4; 2 John 9).

Salvation is provided freely by God through His grace toward us and can only be realized through Jesus Christ, our Savior (John 8:24; Acts 4:12). Despite all our sins, Christ willingly and lovingly died for us (John 3:16; Romans 5:8; Ephesians 2:8). He shed His blood as atonement for our sins (Hebrews 9:11-14).

Salvation, however, is not automatic. It is contingent on believing in Jesus, God's Son and our Savior, repenting or turning away from our sins, confessing faith in Christ and being buried with Him in baptism for the forgiveness of our sins (Matthew 28:19-20; Mark 16:16; Luke 13:3; John 3:5; Romans 6:3-10; 10:9-10; Galatians 3:27; Hebrews 11:6). Finally, salvation has two facets—salvation from past sins and for eternity (1 Peter 1:9; Revelation 2:10).

Muslim Attitude toward Christianity

By now in this study it should be apparent that Islam is totally exclusive. Muslims affirm that the only true faith is Islam. There is absolutely no room for accommodation or pluralism in Islamic mentality. "Islam means everything . . . Islam contains everything. Islam includes everything. Islam is everything" (Ruhollah Khomeini, in a statement to reporters. Cited in Sumrall 1981:119).

Those who do not follow Islam's teachings are rejected by Allah and punished eternally. Those who reject the prophethood and apostleship of Muhammad are unbelievers and destined for eternal Hell (Sûrah 4:150-151). A Hadith from Muhammad reads as follows: "Any Jew or Christ who heard about me and did not believe in me and what was revealed to me in the Holy Qur'an and any traditions, his ultimate destination is the Hell Fire" (Khan n.d., *Translation of the Meanings of Sahih al-Buhhari, al-Medina:* Islamic University, Vol. 1:56-61).

This was not always true, however. At the beginning Jews and Christians were considered People of the Book and capable of receiving salvation, if they followed the teachings of the Book. " . . . those who are Jews, and Christians, and Sabaeans—whoever believeth in Allah and the Last Day and doeth right—surely their reward is with their Lord, and there shall no fear come upon them neither shall they grieve" (Sûrah 2:62). Only later did Jews and Christians come to be considered infidels, and especially since the time of the Crusades, when both Christians and Muslims looked on the other group as pagan. Christianity has been equated with the political systems of the West. Is there any wonder about their hostile attitudes toward those governments labeled as imperialist or colonialist?

Muslim Attitude toward Judgment, Eternal Life, and Punishment

Islam teaches that all humans will be judged by God, but only faithful Muslims will pass after death into Paradise, a perfect physical place where they will have beautiful "dark-eyed virgins" to serve them forever (Sûrah 36). Or, as described in Sûrah 52:19-20, "They will recline on thrones arranged in ranks; and we shall join them to companions with beautiful, big and lustrous eyes."

Christians and Jews, on the other hand, are condemned to the "abode of Fire" because of their belief that "God is Christ the son of Mary" (Sûrah 5:75).

Bridging Two Worlds

The Drawing Table

1. Contrast the views of Islam toward the Bible with those of Joseph Smith or Charles Russell.
2. Where did Muhammad get the name of Allah for God?
3. Could the Gospels be used with Muslims? If so, how? If not, why not?
4. Explain the Muslim misunderstanding of God as three Beings.
5. How do Muslims understand salvation?

Bridge-Building Tools

They say the best defense is a good offense. This is true with evangelism. Write your plan for sharing the gospel with a Muslim based on your study of this book so far. Find ways to write your plan of offense in letters to Muslims or through E-mail.

Plan to attend a lecture or seminar on Christian theology in the next three months. Learn how to explain "the Trinity" to non-Christians.

Sons of Abraham and Sons of God—
the Covenant of Faith

But when the time had fully come, God sent his Son, born of a woman, born under law, to redeem those under law, that we might receive the full rights of sons. Because you are sons, God sent the Spirit of his Son into our hearts, the Spirit who calls out, "Abba, Father" (*Galatians 4:4-6*).

He is the image of the invisible God, the firstborn over all creation. For by him all things were created: things in heaven and on earth, visible and invisible, whether thrones or powers or rulers or authorities; all things were created by him and for him. He is before all things, and in him all things hold together. And he is the head of the body, the church; he is the beginning and the firstborn from among the dead, so that in everything he might have the supremacy. For God was pleased to have all his fullness dwell in him, and through him to reconcile to himself all things, whether things on earth or things in heaven, by making peace through his blood, shed on the cross (*Colossians 1:15-20*).

In the past God spoke to our forefathers through the prophets at many times and in various ways, but in these last days he has spoken to us by his Son, whom he appointed heir of all things, and through whom he made the universe. The Son is the radiance of God's glory and the exact representation of his being, sustaining all things by his powerful word (*Hebrews 1:1-3a*).

By faith Abraham . . . . made his home in the promised land like a stranger in a foreign country; he lived in tents, as did Isaac and Jacob, who were heirs with him of the same promise. For he was looking forward to the city with foundations, whose architect and builder is God. By faith Abraham, even though he was past age—and Sarah herself was barren—was enabled to become a father because he considered him faithful who had made the promise. And so from this one man, and he as good as dead, came descendants as numerous as the stars in the sky and as countless as the sand on the seashore (*Hebrews 11:8-12*).

8

Muslim Family and Community

There is no question in Islam about family solidarity and loyalty. Nor is there any question about loyalty to Islamic community. Although by our standards, it may seem extreme at times, this kind of loyalty could well be emulated in the Western world.

Islamic Family Law

Family law is the core of Islam's social structure. The Qur'an devotes more attention to marriage, women's place in the family and society and the family, as such, than any other subject. The Qur'an, given to a patriarchal tribal world, reflects the Arabian situation of the seventh century and attempts to address the weaknesses in that system. The three basic elements found in Islamic law regarding family life are marriage, divorce, and inheritance.

Regulations about Marriage

Marriage is regarded as a sacred covenant, not a sacrament, with the potential marriage partners chosen by the two respective families. This practice had many ramifications of a tribal, social, and economic nature. It is very much patriarchal in nature, with the husband being the absolute authority in the home.

It is against Islamic law for a Muslim to marry a non-Muslim. Early in its history Islam permitted marriage of a Muslim male to a believer in the Book, but this changed, with Jews and Christians coming to be seen as infidels. Muslim women were never permitted to marry outside of Islam.

Polygamy, which is officially sanctioned, is however controlled. A Muslim man is permitted up to four wives, if he can care for them and their children equally (Surâh 4:3). An interesting side note is that Muhammad had as many as 11 wives, as well as concubines. Strangely enough, this was permitted for him as an exception to the rule: "Prophet! We have made lawful to thee thy wives . . . a privilege for thee only, and not (rest of) believers" (Sûrah 33:50).

Women are given higher status than in pre-Islamic Arabia. Yet, in many Muslim countries women must still remain largely in seclusion and veiled in public, as well as being garbed in a shapeless robe, the *chador*. The news media showed in October 2001 scenes of women being beaten publicly by Taliban enforcers. The fundamentalist Taliban did not even permit a woman to talk above a whisper in public, nor were they permitted to receive an education.

Divorce is permitted, but only for the husband. According to Islamic law, he has the unilateral right to dismiss his wife simply by declaring, "I divorce you." He was supposed to say this three times, a month apart, to confirm that his wife was not carrying a child by him. This was circumvented later by the husband's repeating three times in quick succession his declaration of divorce. Divorce, however, is discouraged, with counsel offered to seek reconciliation of the marriage.

Muslim Loyalty to Family

Family and children are high priorities in Muslim life. The husband expects heirs, especially male. The family is not just nuclear, as in Western society, but is extended. That is, it includes parents, aunts, uncles, and other near relatives. Often, the nuclear family lives with parents and other family members. Family ties are especially strong. This extended family demands great family loyalty and mutual aid. The Muslim who goes his or her own way is considered a threat to the family and its proper continuity.

Muslim Loyalty to Community

Community, first and foremost, is one's own extended family. But community extends also to one's own clan, tribe, and brotherhood of faith. As in sub-Sahara Africa, tribal connections outweigh by all odds a feeling of patriotism toward country. Many of the Islamic countries are arbitrary geographic entities, imposed often by earlier colonial powers or by treaties following wars. Geographic boundaries mean little. Community means everything. Any threat to family, clan, or tribal connections is a threat to the individual.

Community means more to Muslims, however, than his or her own family, clan, and tribe. It involves the entire Muslim community, both local and worldwide. The current war going on in Afghanistan is fraught with political and religious land mines, because any attack on a Muslim country can easily cause many other Muslim countries to rise up in its defense, whether its behavior has been right or wrong. Loyalty to community can become intensely fanatical, as is happening in various parts of the Islamic world today.

The brotherhood of Muslims is reinforced by daily prayers and practicing the other Pillars of the Faith, especially the Pilgrimage to Mecca. There, millions of the faithful go through the rituals in concert. There is, then, a strong relationship between the individual and community, or *ummah* —nothing of the rugged individualism of Americans. " . . . the individual was taken out of his isolation and insecurity and made to feel that he belonged to the ummah . . . . The ummah was a closely-knit community, thought of along the lines of the tribe, and much of the old mystique attaching to the kinship group has become attached to it" (Watt 1961: 301-302).

A Strong Sense of Hospitality

Islam requires that hospitality must be practiced at all times. Even foreigners and the poor must be taken in and treated as family. As strange as it may sound, an American "infidel" walking up to a Muslim family's tent or house is to be invited in and given every consideration. While in that dwelling place as a Muslim's guest, he is under the family's protection. He or she may be killed out on the street, but not in a Muslim's home.

> For the Muslim Arab, friendship involves the expenditure of time and effort; time to be together, to relate to one another, to offer food, to talk. If you are a friend of someone in the Arab world, there is almost no limit to what you might be expected to do. He may only have a few close friends, but these are usually willing to commit their lives, their wealth, their good names for their friend (Kershaw 1979:1).

This sounds strange to us with our lists of many "friends," but few really close friends of the "All for one, one for all" mentality of the Three Musketeers. Our superficiality of friendships and even of family relationships is totally foreign to the Muslim mind.

Muslim Family and Community

Bridging Two Worlds

The Drawing Table

1. What lesson for the West is there in the Islamic view of family?
2. How do Islamic views of marriage compare with those of Christianity?
3. Describe Islamic teaching on divorce. How does this compare with practices in the West?
4. Contrast Christian and Muslim views of community.
5. What is the irony of being an infidel, yet guest, in a Muslim home?

Bridge-Building Tools

Invite a Muslim friend or family to your house for one of your family activities. You might choose to go out to eat together or take in a sporting event.

Plan a trip with your Muslim friends. Schedule to attend a church event whether it be worship or regional gathering. Demonstrate your concern and genuine love for Muslims without compromising your Christian beliefs, or forcing them on your Muslim acquaintances.

Inspired Scriptures, Eyewitnesses, and the Assurance of Salvation

Concerning this salvation, the prophets, who spoke of the grace that was to come to you, searched intently and with the greatest care, trying to find out the time and circumstances to which the Spirit of Christ in them was pointing when he predicted the sufferings of Christ and the glories that would follow. (*1 Peter 1:10-11*).

And we have the word of the prophets made more certain, and you will do well to pay attention to it, as to a light shining in a dark place, until the day dawns and the morning star rises in your hearts. Above all, you must understand that no prophecy of Scripture came about by the prophet's own interpretation. For prophecy never had its origin in the will of man, but men spoke from God as they were carried along by the Holy Spirit (*2 Peter 1:19-21*).

The life appeared; we have seen it and testify to it, and we proclaim to you the eternal life, which was with the Father and has appeared to us. We proclaim to you what we have seen and heard, so that you also may have fellowship with us. And our fellowship is with the Father and with his Son, Jesus Christ (*1 John 1:2-3*).

Who is the liar? It is the man who denies that Jesus is the Christ. Such a man is the antichrist—he denies the Father and the Son. No one who denies the Son has the Father; whoever acknowledges the Son has the Father also (*1 John 2:22-23*).

Anyone who does not believe God has made him out to be a liar, because he has not believed the testimony God has given about his Son. And this is the testimony: God has given us eternal life, and this life is in his Son. He who has the Son has life; he who does not have the Son of God does not have life. I write these things to you who believe in the name of the Son of God so that you may know that you have eternal life (*1 John 5:10b-13*).

9

Terror in Every Tower

Islamic fundamentalist terrorism came home to roost in the U.S. September 11, 2001. The unthinkable happened—the most devastating terrorist attack in all of human history. And we ask ourselves "why?" "Why did it happen?" "Why do they hate us so much?" We are perplexed, angry, and frustrated. We seek answers. This chapter posits some possible responses.

A Matter of Worldview

A fundamental reason for their behavior is in their worldview. As we have said, worldview is the way in which individuals and groups perceive how everything functions. At its heart worldview is made up of assumptions seldom if ever questioned, values, and loyalties. We are not born with these worldview components implanted in our brains. They are acquired from parents, peers, colleagues, schools, business organizations, religions, folklore, local and national mentality, and personal experience.

These basic assumptions, values, and allegiances grow and remain well fixed in our minds, at least until some trauma causes us to re-evaluate them. Fires, floods, tornadoes, hurricanes, earthquakes, droughts, loss of employment, a move to a new location, illness, war, death in the family, a terrorist attack—these and other factors cause us to question the heart of our worldview and seek to adjust it to make more sense.

The Traumatic Effects of Terrorism

Having briefly described worldview and worldview change, let us look at the trauma affecting our entire nation following the terrorist strikes on Manhattan and Washington, D.C.

Several attempts have been made by churches and schools to build a bridge of understanding between the two worlds since September 11. For example, *WorldNetDaily*, January 11, 2002, reported that an increasing number of California school students must attend an intensive course on Islam (ASSIST News Service). Seventh graders must learn the tenets of Islam, study the important figures of the faith, wear a robe, adopt a Muslim name, and stage their own jihad. Students must memorize verses in the Qur'an and are taught to pray "in the name of Allah, the Compassionate, the Merciful, and are instructed to chant, "Praise to Allah, Lord of Creation." (It's one thing to walk a mile in another's moccasins, sandals, or shoes, but perhaps something else to wear another's robe and turban?) Where is the ACLU in times like these? What would happen if Christianity were presented in a similar manner?

Prior to September 11 we had assumed that nothing of a terrorist nature could strike in the heartland of our country. We were wrong. We had assumed that the day of aircraft hijackings was over. Not so, not by a long shot. We had assumed that our oceans and security systems would protect us. We now know that they do not. We were violated in a most horrendous way. We assumed that, since we were living in peace and relative prosperity, nothing like this could ever happen to us. We now know that these assumptions were wrong. We will be forced to adjust them. We will be required to lose some of our individual freedoms to help guarantee the future safety of all. Apparently we will even be forced to handle mail with care, due to the transmission of anthrax through letters and packages.

At the writing of this book, a 34-year-old Pakistani Christian, Ayub Masih, faces a death sentence for blasphemy in praising Salman Rushdie's *Satanic Verses*. His is the first case to reach the Pakistani Supreme Court. This is one of many like circumstances around the world. Beware that law and justice are defined differently in Christian and Muslim contexts.

Why was journalist Daniel Pearl brutalized and murdered? Perhaps in part because he was a journalist from the West. Perhaps because he was accessible to a terrorist group. Perhaps because he was a Jew. And perhaps because he was "collateral damage" for the terrorists. They sought retaliation against the U.S. for the defeat of the Taliban and the damage done to al-Qaeda in Afghanistan. Pearl was just one person, but had a worldwide voice, and if they could destroy him, symbolically they could destroy to some extent the voice of America. *The Wall Street Journal*, of which he was an employee, is America's premier publication on Western economics. The terrorists could give a black eye to the *Journal* and thus to the "decadent" American economic system. *Time* magazine (March 4) suggests another possible reason for Pearl's assassination. It is the writer's belief that this was a way of getting at the president of Pakistan for siding with the West in the war against terrorism.

Recently NBC TV displayed a United States map indicating the location of known Islamic terrorist cells across the country. They exist in almost every major city, including my hometown of Oklahoma City. The authority on terrorism presenting it noted that, unless they are caught engaging in terrorism, there is little that can be done about them, especially if they have legal documentation to be here.

Some Assumptions of the 2001 Terrorists

The terrorists also have basic assumptions, values, and allegiances. Being members of a fanatical cell or cells of the Muslim faith, they assume that what they believe is the only possible way of looking at God and life. They assume that, since Allah demands absolute submission, those who do not submit are infidels and even worse, idolaters. They have no right to live!

In fact, they believe that they are doing Allah a service by ridding the world of infidels. Not only this, they believe that dying for their cause is heroism and will be rewarded with an immediate ticket to Paradise. According to Abdullah al-Araby, "the words 'fight' and 'kill' have appeared in the Qur'an more frequently than the word 'pray'"(2001:16). Considering the total belief system of Islam, the only *logical guarantee* of salvation or eternal security for some Muslims comes from becoming a martyr and killing People of the Book through suicide. Otherwise they are frustrated with a life of works-salvation that can never deliver them.

Because they make these assumptions, they value their particularly violent expression of religious faith and are intensely loyal to Allah, Muhammad, and their own leaders. We may be baffled by their behavior, but to them it is the logical outcome of their worldview. They are angry and frustrated. More normal means of achieving their ends have been essentially, to their thinking, exhausted. There remains only violence and terrorist tactics.

Why Anger Directed at the United States?

But why the U.S. as a major target for their anger? There are a number of reasons. First, we represent leadership of the Western and Christian world. We represent wealth, power, and military might. Arab-American Christian Kahlil Jahshan observes on this point: "The question is not about Islamic beliefs and practices that generate hatred for the 'Christian West,' but about social, economic and political issues in underdeveloped Muslim societies that lead to despair and violence" (from interview hosted by Lindy Adams, *The Christian Chronicle*, November 2001:20).

We represent, to the Islamic mind, the major source of manpower and funding for Christian missions. According to Sumrall, 90 percent of all mission funds and most of missionary personnel in the world come from the United States (1981:117-128).

We represent democracy and freedom, and especially equality for women. These points are anathema to Islam, which, in its ideal form, is theocratic. Individual freedom is exactly the opposite of the total submission required in Islam.

Muslim leaders, therefore, have an abiding fear of the liberation that democracy can bring to peoples.

Moreover, we symbolize secularism and materialism, modernity, globalism, and the universal spread of our culture and language. Our TV programs, radio material, books, magazines, clothing styles, sporting events, eating habits, music, and other facets of our lifestyle are saturating the earth. In The Netherlands, for instance, I recently saw far more Golden Arches than windmills.

McDonalds and Coca Cola can be found throughout China, Nepal, India, and, in fact, essentially all countries. The traditional culture and religion of the Muslim world are therefore seriously threatened by all of this. The ideal lifestyle, to many Muslim leaders, is that of a thousand years ago. Western culture, especially that of the U.S., must be fought to the death. Osama bin Laden, in a televised speech early in October 2001, announced:

> The nations of infidels have all united against the Muslims . . . . This is a new battle, a great battle, similar to the great battles of Islam, like the conquest of Jerusalem . . . . [The Americans] come out to fight Islam in the name of fighting terrorism. These events have split the world into two camps: the camp of belief and the camp of unbelief.

We could easily find ourselves in a black hole, a world war for survival against the fanatical perhaps millions of Muslims who would willingly die for their cause. If other Muslim nations conclude that we are after the people of Afghanistan and their faith, these many nations could turn against us in the blink of an eye and we could see a "Battle of Armegeddon," fought not in the valley of Jezreel in Israel, but in the sands and rugged mountains of the Middle East.

Then there is the political aspect. David Van Blema says that events in Albania and Chechnya, as well as Israel, "create a nationalist desperation. "We side with Israel in conflicts with the Palestinians. We support governments in the Islamic world that are considered heretic or at least clients of the

West. We meddle in Mid-Eastern countries and their affairs. We blockade Iraq and have our strong differences with Iran, Libya, and other Islamic countries. We profane holy ground in Saudi Arabia by the presence of our military personnel. We place on trial and imprison terrorists. To their thinking we are The Great Satan, as Khomeini was fond of saying—the embodiment of all that is evil. We are also a free and open society that, as it turns out, is especially vulnerable to their terrorist attacks.

There is also an intense hatred for non-Muslims, dating back to conflicts involving Ishmael and Esau in Abraham's and Isaac's day, as well as back to the Crusades and to western colonialism. Hazem Saghiyeh, a columnist for the Arabic newspaper *al-Hayat*, courageously writes:

> . . . we in the Muslim world have not been able to overcome the trauma caused by colonialism. We could not open up the tools that modernity suggested, for the simple reason that they were introduced by way of colonialism. Our oil wealth allowed us to import the most expensive consumer commodities, but we could not overcome our suspicions of outside political and ideological goods: democracy, secularism, the state of law, the principle of rights and, above all, the concept of the nation-state, which was seen as a conspiracy to fragment our old empire . . . .
>
> Arab intellectuals, who ought to encourage change, have largely failed in that role. For the most part, they did not detach themselves from the tribal tradition of defending "our causes" in the face of the "enemy." Their priority has not been to criticize the incredible shortcoming that they live with. They tend ceaselessly to highlight their "oneness." Thus they help stereotype themselves . . . . It is in this particular history and this particular culture, and not in any alleged clash of civilizations, that the roots of our wretched present lie (reprinted in *Time*, October 15, 2001).

Mix all of these elements together and nurture them by militant fundamentalist leaders in certain nations. Then stir into the mix the financial resources to accomplish their purposes. The result? Thousands dead in the rubble of Manhattan and the Pentagon. Those hijacking the planes and many others like them willingly sacrifice their lives in the hopes of creating chaos and terror in the ranks of the "infidel" enemy and hopefully even the breakdown of its society.

To illustrate this, among the papers of El Sayyid Nosair, charged with the killing of Rabbi Meir Kahane in New York in 1990, but not convicted, was this statement: "We have to thoroughly demoralize the enemies of God . . . by means of destroying and blowing up the towers that constitute the pillars of their civilization, such as . . . the high buildings of which they are so proud" (cited by columnist George Will in the *Daily Oklahoman*, September 14, 2001). And yet another result: Palestinians celebrated in the streets over the success of their "heroes" against the evil Americans.

A Gallup poll following the terrorist attacks, conducted among nine thousand plus residents from nine countries where about half of the world's Muslim population resides, revealed that most believed that "the United States was aggressive and biased against Islamic values." That "sixty-one percent said they did not believe Arab groups carried out the September 11 terrorist attacks" (CNN.com, February 26, 2002).

Waking a Sleeping Giant

Admiral Yamamoto commented as Japanese planes were bombing Pearl Harbor, "I fear we have only awakened a sleeping giant, and his reaction will be terrible." His words were prophetic and purveyors of mass destruction should have learned a lesson from him. However, they have not. Again, a sneak attack has left ugly gashes on our shores. September 11, 2001 has given us another "Day of Infamy." Again, we as a people will rally to the defense of our nation and will spare no effort to bring to justice those responsible. The giant has once again awakened. Woe be to the perpetrators of this unspeakable crime! Our world is too small, as President George W. Bush has said, for them to find a safe hiding place. Leonard Pitts Jr., columnist for the *Miami Herald*, said this following the terror attacks, speaking to the perpetrators: "Did you want us to respect your cause? You just damned your cause. Did you want to make us fear? You just steeled our resolve. Did you want to tear us apart? You just brought us together" (quoted in *Reader's Digest*, November 2001, p. 61).

Can we expect more terrorism? Certainly. Terrorist cells will not lie still. They will seek retaliation in spades against the West for counter-attacking the Taliban and Osama bin Laden. And the next time their attacks may be even more unthinkable—chemical, germ, or even atomic warfare. We have already seen, on a small scale so far, the use of anthrax to threaten the lives of American media people and government officials.

Christian Response to Terrorism

Our nation undoubtedly will continue to respond in kind to the terrible devastation wrought in Manhattan and our nation's capital. The thud of bombs and the rattle of small arms fire may well be the only kind of response terrorists will understand. But how should we respond as Christians?

• *First,* Jesus said that we should not fear those who can kill the body, but rather HE who can destroy the soul (Matthew 10:28). Since the greatest dimension of the Christian's life is eternal, our days on earth are a prelude. As the song says, "This world is not my home, I'm just 'a passin' through." We certainly should be deeply disturbed by any kind of violence, but not quaking with fear for our own lives. Paul tells us that "to live is Christ and to die is gain" (Philippians 1:21).

• *Second,* We are obligated to pray for the victims' families and loved ones, as well as for our entire nation in such a time of crisis. In fact, the September 2001 terrorist attack has involved the entire world in one way or another. Our prayers should extend to all peoples.

• *Third,* we must even pray for the perpetrators of such heinous acts. This is extremely difficult to do, but we have clear Bible instructions to do just that: "Love your enemies and pray for those who persecute you . . . ." (Matthew 5:44).

• *Fourth,* we must not seek personal revenge against our enemies. "'It is mine to avenge, I will repay,' says the Lord" (Romans 12:19; see also 1 Peter 3:9). Our God knows and in His own good time, He will balance the books of divine justice.

• *Fifth,* we should pursue every possible way to teach terrorists the way of peace in Christ. Yes, we know something of the worldview mentality of terrorists. But do we ever considered that they have never had the opportunity to see *clearly* a better worldview, one based on Jesus Christ? Do they have no peace in their hearts because they have never met the Prince of Peace?

Jesus told us that "in this world you will have trouble. But take heart! I have overcome the world" (John 16:33). Trials and traumas surround us, but we know that our Lord is still in charge and through Him we will overcome.

God has promised us, "The wicked plot against the righteous and gnash their teeth at them; but the Lord laughs at the wicked, for he knows their day is coming" (Psalm 37:12-13). Let us take solace in this promise.

Bridging Two Worlds

The Drawing Table

1. How does worldview explain Islamic behavior?
2. What were some American assumptions about terrorism prior to September 11, 2001?
3. What were some terrorist assumptions?
4. List some reasons Muslims are angry with America.
5. Explain what "waking a sleeping giant" means.

Bridge-Building Tools

Add to your notebook news items from the Internet, magazines, or newspapers that pertain to Christian/Muslim relations. Highlight key faith statements from both worlds that are behind the stories and counter these sentiments with passages from the Bible.

Visit a mosque in the U.S. with other Christians. Ask questions of your guide. Express your interest in knowing more about Islam but that you are secure in your Christian faith. Invite Muslims to attend a church event. Tell the truth in love and communicate the gospel in words and deeds.

Two Worlds Await Their Judge and the King of Kings

Keep yourselves in God's love as you wait for the mercy of our Lord Jesus Christ to bring you to eternal life. Be merciful to those who doubt; snatch others from the fire and save them; to others show mercy, mixed with fear—hating even the clothing stained by corrupted flesh (*Jude 21-23*).

"Behold, I am coming soon! My reward is with me, and I will give to everyone according to what he has done. I am the Alpha and the Omega, the First and the Last, the Beginning and the End. Blessed are those who wash their robes, that they may have the right to the tree of life and may go through the gates into the city. Outside are the dogs, those who practice magic arts, the sexually immoral, the murderers, the idolaters and everyone who loves and practices falsehood.

"I, Jesus, have sent my angel to give you this testimony for the churches. I am the Root and the Offspring of David, and the bright Morning Star." The Spirit and the bride say, "Come!" And let him who hears say, "Come!" Whoever is thirsty, let him come; and whoever wishes, let him take the free gift of the water of life. I warn everyone who hears the words of the prophecy of this book: If anyone adds anything to them, God will add to him the plagues described in this book. And if anyone takes words away from this book of prophecy, God will take away from him his share in the tree of life and in the holy city, which are described in this book. He who testifies to these things says, "Yes, I am coming soon." Amen. Come, Lord Jesus. The grace of the Lord Jesus be with God's people. Amen (*Revelation 22:12-21*).

10

Sharing Christianity with Muslims

This chapter is perhaps the most needed but difficult to achieve of all of the material in this book. It is needed because Islam is militantly evangelistic. It is growing rapidly throughout the world. And it is needed because more than one billion Muslims in the world either do not know Christ or refuse to confess Him as Lord.

It is difficult because we know so little of their worldview or religious/political philosophy. We know so little about how to share our faith with them. And at the heart of the matter, we fear contact with them.

These barriers can be overcome, however. They are being overcome to a small extent in such places as Malawi, Indonesia, northern Ghana, and to a lesser extent in Israel, Egypt, Pakistan, Mali, Chad, Burkina Faso, Albania, and other Muslim countries.

It is my hope that at least some suggestions for approaching Muslims and sharing Christ with them will come out of this concluding chapter.

Direct Confrontation and Discussion

This is the most aggressive of the approaches and is fraught with danger, because it smacks of a debative mentality. Yet it can be used judiciously. Dr. Jack Evans, president of Southwestern Christian College, Terrell, Texas, has conducted two debates, one with a Muslim scholar and the other with a Black Muslim leader. In an analysis of the first debate, his opponent, Jamal Badawi, was overwhelmed by the careful preparation Evans had made (*The Christian Chronicle*, July 1996, p.1). Following the second debate his opponent, Jeremiah Muhammad, left the Black Muslim faith and embraced Christianity (*The Christian Chronicle,* September 1997).

Other debates on Islam have been held in recent years, among these some between Islamic leaders and former leaders who have converted to Christ. One of these was a debate conducted by Michael Nazir-Ali (recorded in *Frontiers in Muslim-Christian Encounter,* Oxford: Regnum Books, 1987). Another was *Christian-Muslim Dialogue,* published by the Kingdom of Saudi Arabia (Maramar, 1984).

Geisler and Saleeb have several chapters devoted to the defense of Christianity and a Christian response to Islam (1993:205-286). These can be applied to each of the distinctive Islamic doctrines.

For any kind of meaningful dialogue with a Muslim, we must know the Islamic faith well. Errors in understanding or word usage will make our discussion hopeless.

Hospitality and Friendship

As has already been pointed out, hospitality and friendship are essential to any relationship with Muslims. They have the idea that Westerners, and especially Americans, are superficial in their friendships and not particularly willing to open their hearts, homes, and kitchens to foreigners. Conversation is vital to them. Kershaw (1971:3) suggests that we may not agree with what they say, and may even argue, but we should not feel compelled to win every argument. "In the Arab world," he says, "disagreements are often a way friendships are tested" (ibid.).

In extending hospitality we must be careful to offer only food and drink that is acceptable to our guest. We must also be discreet, Kershaw says, in our male-female relationships in our guest's presence (Kershaw 1971:23). Among most Muslims, friendships are formed between those of the same sex. They misinterpret the openness of American women, thinking that it means a possible intimate relationship with them.

Another way in which to show hospitality is to invite a Muslim friend to events in which you are involved and especially, Christian events. Demonstrate in a group setting vital Christian faith and practice. Those present can draw out the Muslim with sincere questions and share with him or her what Jesus means in their lives.

Aid in Times of Need or Distress

In northern Ghana American Christians have opened many Islamic areas to the gospel by drilling wells for villages that had no safe and dependable water supply. This is something that Muslim leaders there had never done. It so impressed the villagers that they listened to what the drillers had to say about Christ.

Dropping food, blankets, and medicines to refugees in Afghanistan is meant to indicate that our battle with terrorists and their supporters is not to be construed as hatred for Muslims in general. It isn't yet known how this will play out. Is it enough to counterbalance the military strikes? Are warlords confiscating much of this, preferring to confiscate it than to see it placed in the hands of starving people?

Of course, aid should never be extended with strings attached. Loving care offered in a time of great need can have an impact on others that may cause them to seek a reason for this kindness.

The Contextualized Use of Honor

In his dissertation, *A Contextualized Theology of Honor,* Evertt W. Huffard presents a case for using the Biblical concepts of *kabod, doxa,* and *timē,* all expressions understandable to Muslims as a means of successful dialogue with them (Huffard 1985:iv).

Kabod is a Hebrew word meaning honor, both in the physical and ethical realms. Its physical characteristics can be expressed in such terms as greatness, respect, praise, power, fear and worship. Related concepts are loyalty, blameless-ness, righteousness, holiness, faithfulness, and a good name —all indications of a correct community relationship.

The Greek word *doxa* means glory and the Greek word *timē* means inner worth or social approval. When the Torah was translated into Greek, notes Huffard, *kabod* inherited a split personality between *doxa* and *timē* (Huffard 1985:228). As used by the early church, *doxa* took on such meanings as opinion, the Christian tradition, reputation, a name for God, the nature of God, Christ, the Holy Spirit, angels, praise, wor-ship, honor given to God, honor of men, final reward, popu-larity, and a desire for fame.

In applying these terms to dialogue with Muslims, Huffard argues that what God has done through Christ is for His *doxa*. Christians are to share the redemptive message because God's honor is at stake. Peter indicates this when he says that God's call to all humanity is based on His divine glory or *doxa* (2 Peter 1:3).

Paul defended his going to Gentiles with the message of Christ by arguing that God's honor required it (Romans 9:22-23). It is God's honor and glory that is revealed in Christ (Hebrews 1:1-3).

In a structured society, as are Muslim communities, it is essential to maintain God's honor, which Islamic peoples can appreciate. The argument can then be made successfully that God, who can do all things He wishes to do, in the manner in which He chooses to do them, chose to show to mankind His *doxa* in sending Himself, in the person of His Son Christ, to die for our sins.

Huffard affirms that "a theology of honor [is] a necessity in reconciling Muslims to God through Christ. With a theolo-gy of honor we create new models for communication cross-culturally (Huffard 1985:283). Incidentally, it might also strengthen our rationale for evangelism, since God's honor is at stake. God's will for humanity was not imposed through a unilateral book. He met us in Christ, a person as well as a manifestation of God, and through Him, we were able to know God and be reconciled to Him (John 8:48-55; 10:30; 14:8-14; Romans 5:10).

Utilizing Muslim Practices in a Christian Context

Not only must we present a theology that penetrates Muslim mental barriers, but we must also utilize what we can, as Christians, of Islamic practices. Whoa! What do we mean by that? Just this: We need to contextualize our message—put it into Muslim clothing, so to speak—in order that it will not appear to be so very foreign to them. The story of the *Peace Child* (Richardson 1976) portrays the results that happened when the message of Christ was presented in a manner with which a New Guinea tribe could identify. Cragg states this point in clear terms:

> Is it possible to familiarize the Muslim with the truth that to become a Christian is not a mere shift of communities, that it does not rob Muslim society . . . of a potential servant and the local community . . . of a loving son? How can we demonstrate that to become a Christian is to remain responsible in some sense for "Muslim" citizenship? . . . . What, then, can be done to encourage in Islam the truth that becoming a Christian is not ceasing to belong with Muslim need, Muslim thought and Muslim kin? (Cragg 1985:348).

Understanding Islamic Worldviews

In order to avoid such pitfalls as that above, we must come to understand the basic worldview that ties Muslims together worldwide and also the particular worldview of different Islamic peoples.

By way of review, worldview is defined as the collective assumptions, values, and allegiances that for the core of a person's or group's way of perceiving how everything in the world functions, a people's way of looking at reality (Kearney 1984:41). Our worldview is at the center of all of our understandings, culture, attitudes, and habits.

Basic Islamic worldview assumptions include that of an

all-powerful God, Allah, who arbitrarily laid down rules and practices to follow. Although merciful, He is not necessarily all that loving or forgiving. Salvation consists of living up to a strict code and doing all of the right things in the right way. Allah is one only, so there can be no manifestations of Him in any form, such as Jesus. Muhammad must be honored above all men as Allah's final and greatest Messenger and Apostle. The Qur'an is Allah's final revelation to mankind. No other religion can be tolerated, because they are all pagan. Family and community solidarity are all-important and are based on a common Islamic faith.

Now, with this set of assumptions, it is not surprising that Muslims value highly the Qur'an, Muhammad, the Ahadith, the Five Pillars of the Faith, and community solidarity. Their allegiance is focused on all of these principles above. Any threat or perceived threat against any of these is considered extremely dangerous and must be destroyed at all costs.

There is much that is commendable in all of this. Who among us Christians could not learn from Muslims about more dedication to prayer, a more submissive life, more dedication to our beliefs? Who could not profit from fasting? Who could not give more generously to alleviate the needs of others? Who could not learn to honor and worship God more intensely? Who could not learn more about zeal for His cause? If we understand thoroughly Islamic worldview, we will be better prepared to use it for drawing Muslims to Christ.

Bridging Two Worlds

The Drawing Table

1. What are the dangers in confronting Muslims through debates?
2. Name some specific ways in which to show hospitality to Muslims.
3. How can we meet physical needs in Islamic countries without its appearing to be social gospel?
4. Explain Evertt Huffard's concept of a "theology of honor."
5. List some lessons we can learn from Muslims.

Bridge-Building Tools

Following are some suggestions coming out of this research for bridging the considerable gap with Muslims:

• Find common ground. One suggestion that comes to mind is the analogy of Jesus as the Lamb of God, sacrificed for our sins. In connection with the Pilgrimage, at the end of Ramadan and at other times when a lamb is offered to Allah. Muslims have been known to turn to Christ, when they finally see in Him God's perfect sacrificial lamb.

• Engage in regular prayer five times a day, but not facing Mecca, of course. This could be done standing, kneeling or even bowing to the floor.

• Practice fasting. If in regular contact with Muslims, even fast during Ramadan, for the glory of God and not for show.

• Give generously, especially to the physical and emotional needs of others. Be the first on the scene in a disaster, if possible, to lift the hands of those who are suffering.

• Build caring friendships. Practice ummah (community) with all those about you. Be hospitable, opening your home to guests, both Islamic and non-Islamic. Show them genuine love. Be sensitive to the dietary restrictions of Muslim guests.

• Place great stress on family, both blood family and Christian family.

• Do not divorce. Do everything possible to avoid marital and family strife.

- Be appreciative of the Muslim accomplishments through the centuries. Many of them have been truly impressive.
- Use the Qur'an and other Islamic writings, especially those about Jesus, when you can in discussion with Muslims. While not necessarily agreeing with the content of the Qur'an, show respect for it, because it does contain many good and valid points along with what we must consider its questionable and erroneous points about Christ, the Bible, and Christianity.
- Avoid a spirit of confrontation if at all possible.
- Know Islam better than Muslims know it.
- Show reverence for the Bible. Muslims would never think of underlining or making notations in the Qur'an, nor would they ever think of dropping it or placing it on the floor. Use an unmarked and well-cared-for copy of the Bible in your discussions.
- Give a copy of the Bible to your contact in his or her own language. Show how to read it more effectively. Some suggest starting with Luke as it is less confrontational at the first. John is more direct about Christ's deity and portrays Jesus, from His own lips, in various manners.
- Present the gospel simply and clearly. Avoid difficult terms. If you use them, define them. Answer questions carefully and respectfully. If you don't have an answer, say so and promise to find it. Be a good listener. Find out what your Muslim friend's views are. As Ashurst and Masood (*Compendium on Islam* 1994; Section 2:2) point out, every Muslim has his own brand of Islam. What does your contact know about Islam and Christianity?
- Practice Christian behavior and be sensitive about your Muslim friend's values and loyalties. Paul reminds us not to be the cause of stumbling (1 Corinthians 10:2-33). How easily we can unknowingly portray wrong attitudes or actions. For instance, dress conservatively. Wear no excessive jewelry and definitely no crosses or other Christian symbols when in the company of a Muslim. Do not fraternize with women in public. Be careful in your home setting to avoid outward

demonstrations of love and familiarity with your spouse or a friend of the opposite sex. And certainly avoid any hint of homosexuality, because Muslims abhor it.

• Remember the trauma a Muslim faces in turning to Christ. The convert faces severe hostility. His or her religion, like a totalitarian government, say Ashurst and Masood, encircles every sphere of his or her life. He or she is accused of blaspheming, dishonoring his or her family, and becoming a traitor to the Muslim community. The convert is therefore considered worthy of death and may even face a real death threat. Ashurst and Masood comment on the conversion of a Muslim: "If at all possible tell his (or her) parents, relatives and friends the truth. Show the relatives verses from the Bible that the convert has not blasphemed God. He has not dishonoured his parents and he is not a traitor (Eph. 6:1-4, Co. 3:20, 1 Tim. 4:4, Rom. 14:1-3)" (Ashurst and Masood 1994:11).

Female converts, especially, are in a difficult situation. The man may be cut off from the community. The woman is imprisoned and whipped every day at the times of prayer until she "repents." (See Ashurst and Masood 1994:11 for further details.) Both the potential convert and we must be convinced that Jesus is worth the risk, and it is a risk for all involved. Converts need much loving care and comfort over a long period of time.

• Finally, incarnate Jesus in your life. We serve a risen Savior, a living and triumphant King. Islam offers the world an inanimate book. We offer a living Christ, a divine BEING living in us. We must demonstrate in our lives our Holy Lord. Smith says, "In a spiritual sense, it is all the difference between the written word and the incarnate Word . . . . In Jesus we have a reliable guide in whose footsteps we can confidently follow" (Smith 1992:267).

The apostles were on trial for preaching Christ. Their judges "took note that they had been with Jesus" (Acts 4:13). The Muslim world can take note also that we have been with and are with Jesus, that He lives in us. How, then, will they be able to deny His power and sovereignty in our lives?

Completing the Bridge

We have been through a complex study in this book, yet we have only touched the hem of the very ample Arabian robe that is Islam. We have begun with the Arab world before Muhammad's day. We have outlined his life and his leadership of a new and powerful movement. We have been introduced to the Qur'an. We have studied later Islamic writings and history, divisions in the movement and its present-day status. We have examined its basic tenets of faith and the life and attitude of its followers. We have noted that it is a system primarily of salvation by works.

In a section as new as today's headlines, we have looked at fundamentalist terrorism, its rationale, and the reasons for its hatred of the West. We have seen, frighteningly, that Osama bin Laden and others are doing everything possible to foment another "Crusade" between "the camp of belief and the camp of unbelief."

We have also compared Islam with Christianity. We have shown that Islam can be understood and answered. It is not a monolithic structure, but rather, fragmented. It has serious discrepancies in its system and is facing its own deep dilemmas.

In closing we have given some suggestions for approaching Muslims in an effort to convert them to Christ. Since they do not accept Him as Savior, they are dead in their sins, as Paul told the Ephesian Christians in regard to their former pagan life (Ephesians 2).

If we truly believe that Muslims have no hope of redemption in their present faith, it is incumbent on us as Christians to reveal clearly to them their lost condition and their need for Christ. We also owe God the honor of sharing His message with them. Historically, Christianity has had a very limited presence and impact on the Islamic world. Now with 1.2 billion followers and growing rapidly, this is one of the last great spiritual frontiers, and perhaps the most difficult and dangerous, to be penetrated by Christ and His followers. Perhaps at no time in history has it been more imperative to turn our spiritual enemies into spiritual family.

Remember, always, that the historical goal of Islam, and especially the fundamentalists and terrorist groups, is to dominate the entire world, ridding it of "infidels," and establishing a worldwide theocracy governed by Islamic law. In the case of the fundamentalists, this means returning to a thousand years ago and the repressive regulations governing everyone, especially women.

A brother in Christ, hearing about this manuscript, asked, "Isn't it dangerous to put out a book like this?" I told him that it could well be, but at this point in time, I felt it essential to do so. God grant me the courage to stand up under any criticism or persecution that may arise over it. Samuel Zwemer, a renowned missionary specialist on Islam, said in 1906, "Of course it will cost life. It is not an expedition of ease nor a picnic excursion to which we are called . . . . It is going to cost many a life, and not lives only, but prayers and tears and blood" (quoted in Morgan 1998:devotional reading for April 14).

It is my heartfelt prayer that this book, limited as it is, may be used by the Lord to help stir us up to taking Islam seriously, understanding it better, and preparing for a truly *spiritual* holy war for the souls of its 1.2 billion disciples worldwide. May He allow us to be living sacrifices, not dying martyrs for His cause.

One of the major differences between Muslims and Christians is that some Muslims are intent on sending Christians to Hell while we are intent on introducing Muslims to Jesus as Savior and bringing them with us to Heaven! May the Lord use us in completing the bridge building between two vastly different worlds!

Appendix 1

Key Terms for the Study of Islam

Abu Bakr—a rich merchant of Mecca who was one of the first converts to Islam (He was a close friend and kinsman of Muhammad and was also the first caliph.)

Ahadith—(see Hadith)

Ali—a cousin of Muhammad who married Fatima, the Prophet's daughter (He was the fourth caliph.)

al-Qaeda or al-Qaida—the fundamentalist terrorist network led by Osama bin Laden

Azan or Adhan—daily call to prayer by the muazzins (muezzins)

Caliph or Khalif—title of the spiritual and political leaders who followed Muhammad

Deen—Muslim religious practices

Five Pillars of Islam—the chief duties of Muslims: Recite the creed, pray five times a day, fast during the Month of Ramadan, give alms (religious tax) and make a pilgrimage to Mecca at least once

Hadith (plural Ahadith)—a story; an oral tradition later written down of what the Prophet was said to have stated, did, or approved of

Hajj—pilgrimage to Mecca

Hamas—terrorist group centered in Israel and adjacent regions

Hezbollah—terrorist group centered in Lebanon

Hijra—Muhammad's flight from Mecca to Medina in AD 622, the date used by Muslims to divide all time and begin the Muslim era

Ijma—consent of the community; a decision arrived at by reasoning or analogy and, once determined, has the force of law

Imam—a spiritual leader looked upon by Shiite Muslims as a legitimate descendent of Muhammad and an authority on spiritual matters

Injil—the Gospels as originally given, before their corruption by Christian leaders, according to Muslims; literally "Good News"

Isa (al-Masih)—Arabic word for Jesus (Christ)

Ishmael—first son of Abraham through his wife's maid, Hagar (Muslims believe that the promise of God came through Ishmael, not Isaac.)

Islam—the religion revealed to Muhammad; the word means surrender or submission to the will of Allah

Islamic Jihad—fundamentalist terrorist group centered in Egypt

Jihad—sacred struggle through teaching and/or the sword in Allah's cause; a holy war or struggle

Jinn—a genie or spirit

Ka'bah or Kaa'ba—a cubicle stone building in the court of the mosque in Mecca toward which Muslims pray and around which they circle during their pilgrimage [They touch or kiss the sacred black stone (believed by Muslims to have been built by Abraham) in the corner of the Ka'bah.]

Khadija—Muhammad's wealthy first wife and the first person to believe his message

Mecca—city in Saudi Arabia; the birthplace of Muhammad—considered the most holy city of Islam

Medina (or al-Madina)—the second-most holy city of Islam (It is located to the north of Mecca. Medina is the city to which Muhammad fled in AD 622.)

Minaret—tower of a mosque from which the call to prayer is made five times a day

Muhammad—founder of Islam; born in Mecca around AD 570 and died there in AD 632 (He is believed by Muslims to be Allah's final and greatest prophet.)

Muslim—one who submits to Allah; a follower of Muhammad

Appendix 1: Key Terms for the Study of Islam

Muazzin (or muezzins)—the mosque official who calls the faithful to prayer

Qibla (or Qiblah)—the direction toward Mecca to be facing during prayer

Qur'an—the Holy Scriptures of Islam (Muslims believe it to be the final revelation of God, given by the Angel Gabriel to Muhammad over a period of 23 years. It is thought to be the perfect replica of the original in Heaven.)

Ramadan—ninth month of the Islamic calendar—devoted to fasting in celebration of the Qur'an's first being revealed to humanity

Rasul—an apostle; a title given to Muhammad in the ritualized prayer

Salat—prayer, primarily the five daily ritual prayers required of all Muslims

Saum or Sawm—fasting during the Month of Ramadan

Shahadah—recitation of the Muslim creed ("I declare there is no god but Allah, and I declare that Muhammad is the Messenger of Allah.")

Shari'ah—Muslim religious/political law; the outward path that follows the Qur'an, Ahadith, official tradition, and legal decisions by Islamic jurists over the centuries

Shiites (or Shi'ites)—a major Islamic sect that believes that only Muhammad's son-in-law, Ali, was the true successor of Muhammad (All others through the process of succession are considered usurpers.)

Shirk—association of any other being or entity with Allah (Christians are shirkers, for they place Jesus on a par with God.)

Sufis—a mystical sect of Islam that renounces the world

Sunnah—custom; a way of acting, particularly on the part of Muhammad; written tradition about him

Sunni—the major sect of Islam (Sunnis believe that the true line of succession from Muhammad is through the four caliphs, Abu Bakr, 'Umar, 'Uthman, and 'Ali.)

Sûrah, Sûra or Surat—a chapter in the Qur'an (These total 144 in number, with the longest first in sequence and the shortest at the end; the contents are not historical or in any kind of sequence, except by length.)

Tari'qa—the inner way of meditation espoused by the Sufis

Ulama—principles Muslim scholars arrived at by consensus

Ummah—community in the sense of family, clan, tribe, and Muslim brotherhood

'Umar—early convert to Islam and the second caliph

'Uthman—another early convert and the third caliph

Zakah or Zakat—a religious offering or tax on all of one's goods (Funds raised in this manner are for the poor in the Islamic world.)

Appendix 2

Nations Totally or Predominantly Muslim

Afghanistan—population 23 million, almost totally Muslim (Center of armed battle with al-Qaeda and the Taliban regime.)

Albania—seventy percent of its more than three million people is Muslim

Algeria—more than 29 million people, almost totally Muslim

Azerbaijan—almost eight million people, almost totally Muslim

Bahrain—600,000 people, 100 percent Muslim

Bangladesh—124 million inhabitants, 83 percent Muslim

Brunei—300,000 people, 67 percent Muslim

Burkina Faso—11 million people, 50 percent Muslim

Chad—two million people, 50 percent Muslim

Comoros—600,000 people, 85 percent Muslim

Djibouti—430,000 citizens, 94 percent Muslim

Egypt—almost 64 million people, 94 percent Muslim

Gambia—one and one half million people, 90 percent Muslim

Guinea—seven and one half million, 85 percent Muslim

Indonesia—207 million inhabitants, 87 percent Muslim (largest number in the world)

Iran—66 million, almost totally Shiite Muslim

Iraq—more than 21 million, almost all Sunni Muslim

Ivory Coast—15 million, 60 percent Muslim

Jordan—more than four million, most are Sunni Muslim

Kazakstan—17 million, the majority of whom are Muslim

Kuwait—two million, almost all Muslim

Kyrgyzstan—between four and five million, primarily Muslim

Lebanon—almost four million, 70 percent Muslim

Libya—between five and six million, almost totally Sunni Muslim
Malaysia—20 million people, predominantly Muslim
Maldives—275,000, essentially all Muslim
Mali—275,000, almost totally Muslim
Mauritania—between two and three million, totally Muslim
Morocco—almost 30 million, 99 percent Sunni Muslim
Niger—nine million plus, 80 percent Muslim
Nigeria—104 million, 50 percent Muslim
Oman—more than two million, entirely Muslim
Pakistan—130 million, almost entirely Muslim
Qatar—550,000, 95 percent Muslim
Saudi Arabia—19.5 million, 100 percent Muslim
Senegal—nine million plus, 92 percent Muslim
Sierra Leone—five million, 60 percent Muslim
Somalia—10 million, almost totally Muslim
Sudan—31 million plus, 70 percent Muslim
Syria—15.6 million, 74 percent Muslim
Tajikistan—six million, 80 percent Muslim
Tunisia—nine million plus, 98 percent Muslim
Turkey—62 million, almost exclusively Muslim
Turkmenistan—nine million, almost entirely Muslim
United Arab Emirates—three million, almost all Muslim
Uzbekistan—23 million, mostly Muslim
Western Sahara—almost entirely Muslim
Yemen—more than 13 million, almost totally Muslim, but divided among three sects

The above list contains 47 nations. Other countries with large Muslim populations include Bosnia, Ghana, India, Israel, Singapore, the Philippines, and Trinidad. There is a large number in Canada and the United States (three to four million), as well as in European countries such as England.

Appendix 3

"Was Muhammad a Prophet or Founder of a Human Religion?"

According to Muhammad himself, he was merely an instrument to receive and transmit Allah's true religion. Yet, all that he did in developing Islam fits precisely into the age-long requisites for new religions. A.W. Sadler, consultant to numerous nascent religions, cites 10 requirements for establishing a new religion. Comparison to the life and work of Muhammad is interesting. His 10 points are

• Attack the religious establishment. Ridicule the clergy. Muhammad attacked the priests of the Ka'bah unmercifully and the priests of Mecca in general. Later he also attacked Jewish and Christian leaders.

• Build on old foundations. Use of the Ka'bah for new purposes fits this point.

• You are your teaching. Muhammad was known for an excellent, pleasing personality. He was likened to noble Bedouin ancestry. He was considered the "immaculate model for Muslims."

• Don't write your own scriptures. Muhammad's life is spoken of in the Qur'an, but most of the information by him and about him come in two posthumous sets of traditions called the *Sira* and the *Sunnah*. He himself wrote nothing in the alleged sacred documents. (In fact, it is thought that he was illiterate.)

• Your teaching is therapeutic and you are the medicine. The first teachings of the Qur'an stresses alms for the poor. His devotion as a servant to his people is legendary.

• Never start a religion in a temple town that is also a barracks town. He had his initial success in Medina, a strictly commercial and temple town.

• Find an established, but obscure, holy place.

Muhammad first used Medina, which fits this description. His meditations in obscure caves were an important part of his religion.

• Have two separate sets of disciples. Muhammad had an inner circle in the earliest stages of his movement as well as did his successor, Abu Bakr. Muhammad had a wider circle of disciples whom he sent out to practice social justice.

• Marry well and especially well off. His wife Khadija was an important early convert and a financial and social asset to his cause.

• Good food is good religion. Little has been said on this point in the sources, but eating to establish covenants was well known both in Israel and Arabia.

In summarizing, the cause initiated by Muhammad basically follows Sadler's rules, although he lived far earlier than Sadler. This points to the human-centeredness of Muhammad's movement.

(The material in this appendix was provided by Dr. William Jones, retired professor of religion at Oklahoma Christian University, Oklahoma City, Oklahoma.)

Resources

Abdul-Haqq, Abdiyah Akbar. *Sharing Your Faith with a Muslim.* Minneapolis: Bethany Fellowship, Inc., 1980.

Adams, Lindy. "A Conversation with Kahlil Jashan." *The Christian Chronicle,* November 2001, p. 20.

Ahmed, Akbar S. *Islam Today.* London: I.B. Tauris, 1999.

al Araby, Abdullah. *Islam Unveiled.* 8th Ed. Los Angeles: The Pen vs. the Sword, 2001.

Ali, Abdullah Yusuf. *The Meaning of the Holy Qur'an.* Beltsville, MD: Amana Publications, 1995.

Ashurst, Allare, and Steven Masood. Compendium on Islam. Manchester, England: Jama'at al Masih, 1994.

Beverley, James A. *Christ and Islam: Understanding the Faith of the Muslims.* Joplin, MO: College Press, 1997.

_____. "Islam a Religion of Peace?" *Christianity Today,* Vo. 46. No. 1. (Jan. 7, 2002), p. 32.

Caner, Ergun Mehmet and Emir Fethi Caner. *Unveiling Islam: An Insider's Look at Muslim Life and Belief.* Grand Rapids: Kregel, 2002.

Caskey, Guy V. *A Reply to a Moslem.* Arlington, TX: Mission Printing, Inc., n.d.

_____. *Why Not Be a Moslem?* Arlington, TX: Mission Printing, Inc., 1991.

Cragg, Kenneth. *The Call of the Minaret.* New York: Oxford University Press, 1964.

_____. *Muhammad and the Christian.* London: Darton, Longman and Todd, 1984.

_____. *Jesus and the Muslim: An Exploration.* London: George Allen & Unwin, 1985.

Chavez, Linda. "A Need to Define the Real Enemy." *The Daily Oklahoman,* Oct. 10, 2001.

Davidson, Lawrence. *Islamic Fundamentalism.* Westport, CT:Greenwood Press, 1998.

Donahue, John J., and John L.Esposito. *Islam in Transition: Muslim Perspectives.* Oxford: Oxford University Press, 1982.

Dyer, Gwynne. "A Writer's Folly (and bin Laden's)." A London-based Column. Reprinted in *The Daily Oklahoman,* Oct. 11, 2001, p. 6A.

Eisenberg, Daniel. "Osama's Top Brass." *Time,* Oct. 8, 2001.

Ellwood, Robert S. *Many Peoples—Many Faiths.* Upper Saddle River, NJ: Prentice Hall, 1982.

Esposito, John L. *Unholy War: Error in the Name of Allah.* New York: Oxford University Press, 2002.

_____. *Islam: The Straight Path.* New York: Oxford University Press, 1998.

Frank, Mitch. "A Wealthy Clan and its Renegade." *Time,* Oct. 8, 2001.

Geisler, Norman L., and Abdul Saleeb. *Answering Islam: The Crescent in the Light of the Cross.* Grand Rapids: Baker, 1993.

Gragg, Kenneth. *The House of Islam.* Belmont, CA: Dickinson Publishing Co., 1969.

Huffard, Evertt W. *Thematic Dissonance in the Muslim-Christian Encounter: A Contextualized Theology of Honor.* Pasadena, CA: Fuller Theological Seminary, 1985.

Jones, William E. *The Life of Muhammad.* An unpublished paper. Oklahoma City: Oklahoma Christian University, n.d.

Khalifa, Rashad. *The Computer Speaks: God's Message to the World.* Tucson, AZ: Mosque of Tucson, 1987.

Kearney, Michael. *World View.* Novato, CA: Chandler & Sharp Publishers, Inc., 1984.

Kershaw, R. Max. *How to Share the Good News with your Muslim Friend.* Colorado Springs: International Students, Inc., 1978.

Lammens, H. *Islam: Beliefs and Institutions.* London: Frank Cass & Co., 1968.

Lippman, Thomas W. *Understanding Islam.* New York: Penguin Books, 1990.

Ludwig, Theodore M. *The Sacred Paths.* Upper Saddle River, NJ Prentice Hall, 1996.

Machatschke, Roland. *Islam: The Basics.* Valley Forge, PA: Trinity Press International, 1995.

Resources

Mirza, Muhammad, ed. "Message of Prophets (Sau) Seerah." Speech by Sijed Abul Aaha Muadoodi. E-mail: mmirza@ee.eng.ohio-state.edu, 1992.

Morgan, Robert J. *From This Verse: 365 Inspiring Stories about the Power of God's Word.* Nashville: Thomas Nelson, 1998.

Nasr, Seyyed Hussein. *Islamic Life and Thought.* Albany, NY: State University of New York Press, 1981.

Nazir-Ali, Michael. *Frontiers in Muslim-Christian Encounter.* Oxford: Regnum Books, 1987.

Neusner, Jacob. *World Religions in America.* Louisville, KY: Westminster/John Knox Press, 1994.

Noss, David S. and John B. *A History of the World's Religions.* New York: McMillan College Publishing Co., 1994.

Parshall, Phil. *Beyond the Mosque: Christians within Muslim Community.* Grand Rapids: Baker, 1985.

_____. *Understanding Muslims in Community through Their Traditions.* Grand Rapids: Baker, 1994.

Pitt, Leonard Jr. Editorial in Miami Herald, cited in *Reader's Digest,* November 2001.

Plander, C.G. *The Mizanu'l Haqq.* Austria: Light of Life Press, 1986.

Regensburger, Linda, ed. "The Crescent and the Cross." *Theology News and Notes.* Pasadena, CA: Fuller Theological Seminary, March 1992.

Richardson, Don. *Peace Child.* Glendale, CA: Regal Books, 1974.

Ruthven, Malise. *Islam in the World.* Oxford: Oxford University Press, 1984.

Saghiyeh, Hazem. "It's Not All America's Fault." *Time,* Oct. 15, 2001.

Saal, William J. *Reaching Muslims for Christ.* Chicago: Moody Press, 1993.

Schimmel, Annemarie. *And Muhammad Is His Messenger.* Chapel Hill, NC: The University of North Carolina Press, 1985.

Shipp, Glover. *Análise de Doutrinas.* São Paulo, Brazil: Centro de Estudios Bíblicos, 1985.

_____. "Class Notes on Islam." Course on World Religions. Unpublished, 1992.

_____. "The Islamic World." *The Christian Chronicle,* Vol. 54, No. 7, 1997.

Shorrosh, Anis A. I*slam Revealed: A Christian Arab's View of Islam.* Nashville: Thomas Nelson, 1988.

Smart, Ninean. *The Religious Experience.* Upper Saddle River, NJ: Prentice Hall, 1996.

Sox, David. *The Gospel of Barnabas.* London: George Allen & Unwin, 1984.

Sumrall, Lester. *Jihad: The Holy War.* Tulsa, OK: Harrison House, 1981.

Swartz, Merlin L., Trans. *Studies on Islam.* Oxford: Oxford University Press, 1981.

Swisher, Clarice, Ed. *The Spread of Islam.* San Diego: Greenhaven Press, 1999.

Talmage, Eric. "From Mecca to Jakarta." Associated Press release, Oct. 12, 2001.

Tisdall, W. St. Clair. *The Source of Islam.* Edinburgh: T. & T. Clark, n.d.

Tolson, Jay. "Struggle for Islam." *U.S. News and World Report,* Oct. 15, 2001.

Watt, W. Montgomery. *Bell's Introduction to the Qur'an.* Edinburgh: Edinburgh University Press, 1970.

_____. *Islam and Christianity Today.* Routledge & Kegan Paul, 1983.

Welch, Alford T., and Pierre Cachia. *Islam: Past Influence and Present Challenge.* State University of New York, 1979.

White, Tom, ed. "Worshipping the Same God?" November 2001:3-4. Bartlesville, OK: The Voice of the Martyrs.

Woodberry, J. Dudley, ed. *Muslims and Christians on the Emmaus Road.* Monrovia, CA: MARC, 1989.

Yusseff, M.A. *The Dead Sea Scrolls, The Gospel of Barnabas and the New Testament.* Indianapolis: American Trust Publications, 1985.

Encyclopedias

The Oxford Encyclopedia of the Modern Islamic World, Vol. 1:
76-77.
Funk and Wagnalls New Encyclopedia. 1986: Vol.14.

Additional Resources

Beverley, James A. *Understanding Islam.* Nashville: Thomas
Nelson, 2001.
Braswell, George W. *Understanding Sectarian Groups in
America.* Rev. Ed. Nashville: Broadman & Holman, 1994.
_____. *Islam.* Nashville: Broadman & Holman, 1996.
Emerick, Yahiya. J.A. *The Complete Idiot's Guide to
Understanding Islam.* Indianapolis: Alpha Books, 2002.
(Written from the perspective of a former American
Christian who became a Muslim.)
George, John. *Operation Crescent Moon: Underground
Christians Reaching Muslims in the Land of Mohammed.*
Caney, KS: Pioneer Book Company, 1999.
Rahman, Fazlur. *Islam.* Chicago: University of Chicago Press,
1979.
Schulze, Reinhard. *A Modern History of the Islamic World.* New
York: New York University Press, 2001.
Valentin, Radu. *Jesus, Friend to Terrorists.* Bartlesville, OK:
Living Sacrifice Book Company, Voice of the Martyrs,
1995.

Web sites

www.answering-islam.org.uk (Christian source)
www.gmi.org (Global Mapping International)
www.islamreview.com
www.muhaddith.org (Islamic source)
www.persecution.com //E-mail: thevoice@vom-usa.org

Other

Stay informed concerning global Christian martyrdom in general with

The Voice of the Martyrs
PO Box 443
Bartlesville, OK 74005
(918) 337-8015; fax (918) 338-0189;
orders (800) 747-0085

World Bible School (Internet)
1259 Chariot Circle
Abilene, TX 79602
(915) 673-3916; E-mail: teachers@wbschool.net

Eastern European Mission and Bible Foundation
P.O. Box 90755
Houston, TX 77290
(800) 486-1818; fax (281) 440-1995;
E-mail: fdfarr@aol.com

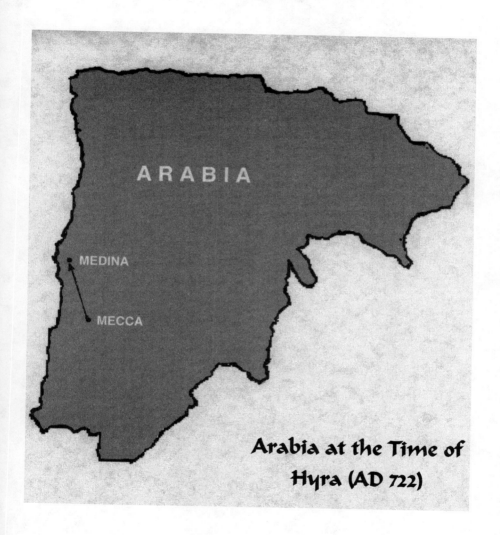

MEDINA

MECCA

Arabia at the Time of
Hyra (AD 722)

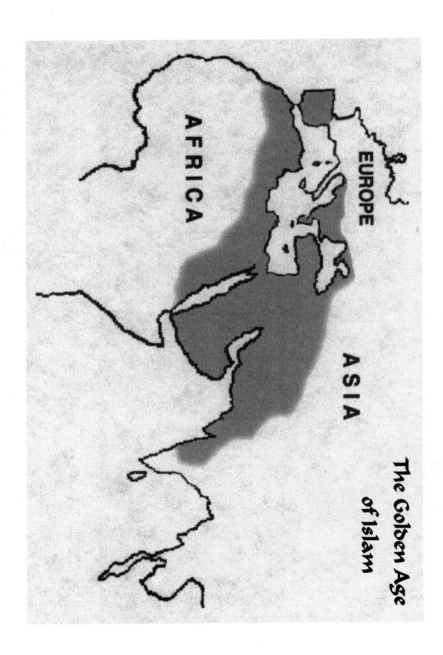

AFRICA

EUROPE

ASIA

The Golden Age of Islam

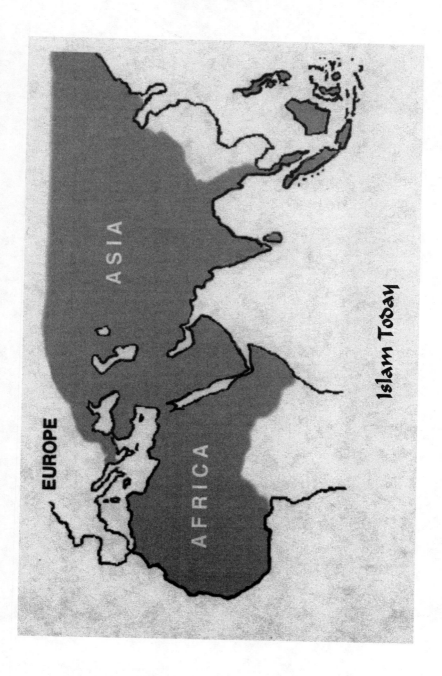

EUROPE

ASIA

AFRICA

Islam Today

135

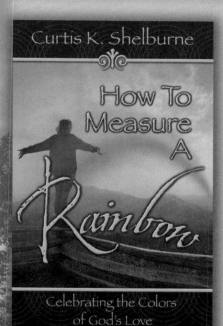

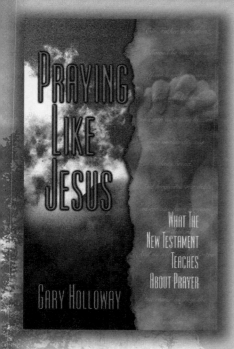